Using Nonfiction for
Civic Engagement in Classrooms

Using Nonfiction for Civic Engagement in Classrooms

Critical Approaches

Edited by Vivian Yenika-Agbaw,
Ruth McKoy Lowery, and Paul H. Ricks

ROWMAN & LITTLEFIELD
Lanham • Boulder • New York • London

Published by Rowman & Littlefield
A wholly owned subsidiary of
The Rowman & Littlefield Publishing Group, Inc.
4501 Forbes Boulevard, Suite 200, Lanham, Maryland 20706
https://rowman.com

Unit A, Whitacre Mews, 26-34 Stannary Street, London SE11 4AB, United Kingdom

Copyright © 2018 by Vivian Yenika-Agbaw, Ruth McKoy Lowery, and Paul H. Ricks

All rights reserved. No part of this book may be reproduced in any form or by any electronic or mechanical means, including information storage and retrieval systems, without written permission from the publisher, except by a reviewer who may quote passages in a review.

British Library Cataloguing in Publication Information Available

Library of Congress Cataloging-in-Publication Data

Includes bibliographic references.
ISBN 978-1-4758-4232-6 (cloth : alk. paper)
ISBN 978-1-4758-4233-3 (pbk. : alk. paper)
ISBN 978-1-4758-4234-0 (electronic)

∞ ™ The paper used in this publication meets the minimum requirements of American National Standard for Information Sciences Permanence of Paper for Printed Library Materials, ANSI/NISO Z39.48-1992.

Printed in the United States of America

Dedication

For Kathy G. Short, whose mentoring knows no bounds! Thank you. May you continue to be blessed to create possibilities for every learner! (Vivian)

For my dad, Henry J. McKoy, Sr. Your life has been a tapestry, a testament of strength, to your children. (Ruth)

For Tim and Myra, two of my favorite humans. (Paul)

Contents

List of Figures		ix
List of Tables		xi
Preface		xiii
Acknowledgments		xv
1	Critical Conversations: Approaches Some Authors Have Adopted to Address Social Issues *Vivian Yenika-Agbaw*	1
2	You, Too, Can Make a Difference: Young Civil Rights Activists *Terrell A. Young, Barbara A. Ward, and Deanna Day*	13
3	Advocating for Immigrant Experiences in Nonfiction Literature *Ruth McKoy Lowery, Kathleen Colantonio-Yurko, and Cody Miller*	25
4	Teaching for Social Justice: Nonfiction Texts and Multigenre Writing *Ann Berger-Knorr and Mary Napoli*	39
5	Sixth Graders' Inquiry into the World War II Japanese Internment Camps *Yoo Kyung Sung and Junko Sakoi*	53
6	Critical Conversations Using Native American Autobiographies *Paul H. Ricks*	69
7	Biographies as Bibliotherapy: Using Nonfiction to Help Boys Overcome Bullying *Lunetta M. Williams and Kelly C. Scott*	83

8	Creating Spaces for Critical Conversations on Issues of Social Justice *Mary Ellen Oslick, Terri Robertson, and Melissa Parks*	95
9	Helpful Resources to Engage Children in Conversations on Social Issues in Nonfiction Literature *Suzanne Chapman, Mario Worlds, and Soowon Jo*	107

Appendix A: A Framework for a Curriculum That Is International	117
Appendix B: Know, Want to Know, Learned Chart Example	119
Appendix C: Graffiti Board Example	121
Appendix D: Graffiti Board Example	123
About the Editors	125
About the Contributors	127

List of Figures

Fig. 2.1	Critical Literacy Questions from Dutro, Kazemi, and Balf (2005).	18
Fig. 2.2	Tableau Directions (Hertzberg, 2003).	20
Fig. 4.1	Student Examples of Multi-genre Projects. Students in the study.	46
Fig. 4.2	Student Examples of Multi-genre Projects. Students in the study.	47
Fig. 6.1	Same Facts, Different Stories.	74
Fig. 6.2	Answer my question with a question.	77
Fig. 6.3	Other Objects to See and Use "Other" Ways.	80
	A Frame Work for Curriculum That Is International. *Bookbird: A Journal of International Children's Literature*, 47(2): 1–10.	117
	KWL Chart example.	119
	Graffiti Board example: Students wrote/sketched their connections, surprises, and questions while reading nonfiction and fiction texts. The sixth grade class.	121
	Students are writing and sketching their responses on Graffiti Board while reading *A Diamond in the Desert*. The sixth grade class.	123

List of Tables

Table 1.1	Authors Who Won the First Nonfiction Book in Each Category or Awards in All Three Major Categories of Interest.	10
Table 3.1	Teaching Suggestions for Expanding Classroom Discussion	31
Table 5.1	Children's Books about Japanese Internment Camps	58
Table 5.2	Timeline in Japanese Internment Camp Unit	60
Table 5.3	Situating Myself through "Where I'm From" Poem	63

Preface

Many who are familiar with our work have come to understand that we are very passionate about issues of social justice and children's literature. And so it would come as no surprise that our book focuses on social issues in nonfiction. Social issues, we also know, present serious challenges to educators.

They make for difficult conversations with teacher candidates, and of course with young children and adolescents whom these future teachers would have to nurture. Because of this, we have also come to understand that several educators tiptoe around certain subjects encountered in literary texts. Perhaps not because they do not think that the subjects are important; rather, because many do not know how to facilitate conversations on these topics.

The purpose of this book, then, is to illustrate how social issues are interwoven in nonfiction literature and other nonfiction texts, and to share possible ways educators might guide students to engage these issues critically. Some may wonder why they should bother with nonfiction, since the information and/or narrative on which the text might be based stems from history or from science. From our experiences teaching children's and adolescent literature in teacher education programs, we have realized that teacher candidates and some in-service teachers are wary of nonfiction texts as tools for literacy.

While these professionals are able to engage in conversations about social issues in fictional narratives, when it comes to nonfiction, they are a bit hesitant, especially when these texts are written and/or produced by members of the said culture—insiders/members of the culture or scientists in the field. First, is the genre not based on fact? Secondly, if written by members who have experienced the cultural, natural, and/or scientific phenomena, should the material not be accepted as accurate?

Using a workshop format in our methods courses, we continue to try hard to alleviate these fears and to dispel the myths of nonfiction simply being the opposite of fiction. Teacher candidates who have passed through our methods courses are quite appreciative of this, especially as they struggle to mediate conversations on difficult subjects with young learners.

We have also come to recognize that when they are equipped with appropriate pedagogical tools, in addition to their sound cognitive background on the subject, these teacher candidates are able to transform conversations on any topic into new learning experiences. We hope readers will be inspired by the exciting stories about the contributors' inquiries on nonfiction texts, and understand that with proper guidance children can develop, and are capable of developing, the necessary skill set and attitude that might enable them to better tackle issues of social justice in all kinds of texts, of which nonfiction is only one. The ability to participate in critical conversations on difficult issues would enhance these children's civic engagements.

OVERVIEW OF THE BOOK

There are nine chapters in this book, including the introduction. Chapter 1 presents different approaches authors of nonfiction texts have employed to address social issues. Chapter 2 discusses nonfiction works that showcase young people's participation in civil rights to reiterate the point of civic engagement at any age. Chapter 3 draws attention to two educators' inquiry on nonfiction texts that explore immigration issues and the value of engaging these issues in a literacy classroom.

Chapter 4 is an inquiry on the use of multigenre writing responses to issues of social injustice. Chapter 5 shares the story of an inquiry with sixth graders to reflect on the larger ramifications of the Japanese Internment Camps in the United States and the role that Japan played during World War II outside of the continental United States. Chapter 6 takes an inquiry stance toward Native American autobiographies to reiterate the point of texts written by insiders to also be critically examined. Chapter 7 explains how bibliotherapy using nonfiction texts on the social issue of bullying can serve young male victims.

Chapter 8 discusses findings from an inquiry on what is considered a safe space for critical dialogue and the challenges faced by graduate students in creating such spaces. Chapter 9 offers helpful resources to facilitate conversations on social issues in nonfiction texts. We hope ideas shared in these chapters inspire educators to continue to tackle, instead of ignore, social issues in *all* texts, to aspire to teach for social justice, and to commit to critical inquiry.

Acknowledgments

This professional contribution would not have been possible without the support of our families, friends, colleagues, administrators, and the interlibrary loan staff at The Pennsylvania State University, who made sure we had access to the relevant professional resources in a timely manner. In addition, a special thank you goes to Tom Koerner, whose faith in the project and constant encouragement kept us focused, and to the Rowman and Littlefield production and editorial team, especially Carlie Wall and Emily Tuttle, for their guidance throughout the project.

We thank the reviewers whose constructive feedback helped to make this project a reality. A book is nothing without the dedication of the authors; thus, we thank all the contributors who worked diligently on their chapters and responded in a timely manner to editorial reminders to bring this project to fruition.

We are thankful to the students whose writing samples and artifacts are included in this book, and wish that all their dreams come true. Additionally, we wish to thank Barbara Lehman, Janet Wong, and Gail V. Ritchie for agreeing to write blurbs for this book at short notice.

Chapter One

Critical Conversations

Approaches Some Authors Have Adopted to Address Social Issues

Vivian Yenika-Agbaw

In an interview for Reading Rockets, Aronson remarks:

> [W]hen we look at any nonfiction . . . whether it's an encyclopedia entry or a vitriolic op-ed, there is a person who wrote it, and that person wrote it from a particular stance. They had an objective, they had a voice, they had a reason for writing about it in that way. And so, when you look at nonfiction, it's not as if there is this perfect truth out there that we channel and absorb and regurgitate.
>
> There are arguments. There are contentions. There are points of view that we come to recognize, that we juxtapose one against the other, that we compare and contrast, and that out of that process we begin to develop our own argument, our own contention. ("Evidence and Nuance in Nonfiction Text": http://www.readingrockets.org/books/interviews/aronson/transcript).

This statement, which at once celebrates the power of nonfiction storytelling while articulating its pluralistic rhetoric, echoes the critical ethos this second volume continues to maintain. To illustrate the point, perhaps it helps to compare two books that reconstruct transatlantic slavery for youth, albeit, moments of this historical event: Linda Gransfield's (1997) *Amazing Grace: The Story of the Hymn*, and Marc Aronson and Marina Budho's (2010) *Sugar Changed the World: A Story of Magic, Spice, Freedom, and Science*.

The choice of these two texts is deliberate, because the human stories they tell emanate from global encounters with this editor's continent of origin. Following are some observations on the authorial stances and how they shape the narrative reader's encounter.

GRANFIELD'S *AMAZING GRACE:* THE STORY OF THE HYMN

Many of the undergraduate students who took a "methods" course with this editor between the late 1990s and mid-2000s were familiar with the popular hymn "Amazing Grace," though very few could associate it with slavery. At Bloomsburg University, where I first introduced the book, a biography of John Newton, some students were so touched by its redemptive message that they were led to share the picture book with members of their church communities. Most later related that it had transformed them in significant ways and altered how they listened to the hymn at funerals and during church services.

I always opened with a read-aloud of the story, followed by profound discussions that enabled the class to reflect further on the issues with which the author grappled and the rhetorical strategies both the author and illustrator employed in telling Granfield's version of a story about slavery. Depending on the group of students, reactions always varied, with some feeling utterly betrayed and others shocked, especially as further research revealed how the Ku Klux Klan (Brummel, 1998) has appropriated the popular hymn.

Our beautiful town at the time was healing from an attempted recruitment endeavor by the Klan that had occurred a couple of years earlier by members of the aforementioned group. The strong emotional and intellectual responses the story elicited from the group of students at the first institution where the book was introduced motivated me to share it with teacher candidates at my current institution.

The reactions were similar, although none mentioned sharing it with members of their church, as was the case at the last institution. In this way, one can infer that the picture book biography of John Newton does have some subversive tendencies. The point of departure for Granfield is her focus on "an ordinary Christian hymn [that] captures the consciousness of an entire historical period" (Yenika-Agbaw, 2006, p. 354). As noted in an earlier article on the book, it quietly lures young readers into thoughtful conversations about slavery, religion, and capitalism, issues that continue to impact present-day society.

But her slightly updated edition, now titled *Out of Slavery: The Journey to Amazing Grace* (2009), opens new conversations about slavery as a brand in children's book publishing. It centers slavery on the front cover, conveying plainly that though a biography of John Newton, the book is about transatlantic slave trade. If one considers Aronson's argument above that authors write nonfiction from a "particular stance," there is no denying that Granfield and Wilson's shifts from religion at the center, as evident on the front cover of the first edition and the blurb on amazon.com, may be motivated partly by the market forces and changing times. The blurb reads:

The hymn's composer, John Newton, led a successful life as a seafaring trader, sailing from Liverpool to Africa and on to Antigua. His cargo was a lucrative one, for he traded in human beings. It was the height of the slave trade, and he made his terrible journey many times. But one night a storm raged. His ship was almost lost. He prayed that if only salvation would come to "a wretch like me," he would leave the slave trade and work towards its abolition.

That night was a turning point in Newton's life. He became an ardent abolitionist and a Methodist minister. But his greatest legacy is "Amazing Grace." (n.p.)

This unique book is an excellent introduction to the history of slavery and also contains the original text of the hymn, music, and map endpapers.

Compare this to the blurb of the updated edition:

> The story of slavery, a man, and the world's most beloved hymn.
>
> John Newton led a rich life. He was a God-fearing man and a successful seafaring trader; his cargo was a lucrative business, for his wares were human beings. In 1748, Newton's ship, the *Greyhound*, sailed the triangular trade route from Liverpool to Africa and on to Antigua as it had many times before. But on one journey, at the height of the slave trade, a storm raged. Feeling all was lost, Newton prayed that if he were spared, he would leave the cruel world of slave trading behind forever. That night, Newton's prayers were answered, and true to his word, he turned his back on the slave trade. In fact, he went on to become an ardent abolitionist. Among Newton's many achievements, his greatest legacy would be the most beloved hymn of all: "Amazing Grace." (n.p.)

Such changes, though seemingly minor, can generate critical conversations among communities of readers within the public school and college settings, and among other local agencies that mediate conversations on important topics in children's literature with young readers. Two examples of such communities in the Washington, District of Columbia, area include the Library of Congress Young Readers' Center and the Smithsonian Museum of African Art.

Across the nation, there are similar communities, especially with the #weneeddiversebook movement, which has raised more awareness about the importance of multicultural children's literature in the school curriculum.

In the National Council of Teachers of English September 2016 *The Council Chronicle*, several educators, myself and Ruth included, were interviewed on the state of multicultural children's literature in the curriculum. Esteemed scholar/educator Violet Harris postulates in that volume that,

> the nonfiction book, *Sugar Changed the World* . . . is unlike other books for young people in its unvarnished depiction of the horrors of slavery. [And that] we don't want to talk about the horrific nature of slavery with children so as a

consequence, we get books that focus on an itty-bitty teeny component of it and sort of humanizes the slave owner and the institution. (p. 14)

While I may not place Granfield's (1997) picture book in the "itty-bitty teeny" category, from this reader's stance the text does seem sympathetic toward John Newton, the "loose packer" (unpaged). This is undoubtedly a conversation that needs to be had within "safe" spaces—in and out of institutionalized settings, and mediated with skill to foster deeper understandings of the ramifications of slavery on a global scale—that is, a slaver who has deep religious convictions and subsequently becomes an abolitionist.

ARONSON AND BUDHO'S
SUGAR CHANGED THE WORLD

As explained in the prologue, the project emanates from the personal lives of the husband and wife team. However, from the personal spaces of its origin, the story morphs into a phenomenal narrative of greed, capitalism, and social injustice on a global scale. The authors assert that, "In fact, while sugar was the direct cause of the expansion of slavery, the global connections that sugar brought about also fostered the most powerful ideas of human freedom" (p. 8).

Broken down into parts, with each highlighting the histories of sugar and human trafficking and the market forces behind this practice that disrupted local, regional, and global communities, and a chapter on the research process, the story spans centuries, shedding light on the complex nature of slavery. In the end, one wonders, as a teacher candidate in my methods course had sighed, "for sugar?" A quick glance at the hundreds of comments on goodreads.com confirms this response.

The comprehensive nature of this illustrated book for early/adolescent readers lends itself to transdisciplinary conversations that hold each reader accountable for *our* being as we struggle to make the world better.

For as Henry Giroux (2016) arguably observes:

> Collective self-delusion will only go so far in the absence of an education system that offers a space for critical learning and dissent, and functions as a laboratory for democracy. There is a tendency to forget in an age dominated by the neoliberal celebration of self-interest and unchecked individualism that public goods matter, that critical thinking is essential to an informed public and that education at the very least should provide students with unsettling ruptures that display the fierce energy of outrage and the hope for a better world. (n.p.)

In this nonfiction book, the slavery component is not swept under the rug; rather, it is presented as part of a chain of events that are linked to human desire for sugar—"tiny crystals stirred into our coffee, twirled on top of a cake" (p. 6). This greed that furthers capitalistic tendencies continues to haunt twenty-first-century society; however, it is the authors' approach to the subject that might quietly remind readers of their complicit roles in this business of human trafficking.

Aronson and Budho interpret historical facts through a narrative lens that reveals the raison d'etre of sugar as their point of entry into this conversation about slavery. Thus, while based on facts, *Sugar Changed the World* is also value laden. The linguistic aspects of the text are interwoven in ways that conjure specific images in a reader's mind about globalization and its exploits. Selective visual historical artifacts that purport to add more credibility to their version of the slave narrative then reinforce these imagined images.

With major parts of the book introducing titles and subheadings that include "From Magic to Spice" (p. 9), "Hell" (p. 31), "Freedom" (p. 71), "A Cycle of Death and Sweetness" (p. 35), and "Slavery or Freedom? The In-Between" (p. 108), and statements such as, "Between the 1600s and the 1800s, sugar drove the entire economy linking Europe, Africa, Asia, and the Americas" (p. 35), the authors' ideology is steeped in the narrative just as in the case of Granfield's *Amazing Grace*.

This ideology can work to manipulate readers' emotions and responses in significant ways. Students then are encouraged not only to read to understand the historical content about slavery and its ties to sugar, but also to reflect deeply on the rhetorical devices that are employed to make this narrative on sugar, empire building, and slavery appear so real.

In addition to investigating the accuracy of facts presented in the book and the authenticity of the maps that accompany the verbal text, they could also be encouraged to ask questions about gaps noticed in the story. For instance, what other plantations existed between the 1600s and 1800s in colonial America? Mediated by an enabling adult, a critical approach to this nonfiction book may generate rich experiences from an interdisciplinary perspective that create opportunities to further understand our social history of inequality, the science behind sugar making, and the complex reasoning behind European navigation of other worlds and/or seafaring.

Such critical conversations are made possible by educators willing to engage students in inquiry about our world, especially in these times when there is pressure to simply consume and regurgitate information at all spectrums of the educational institution. We must rethink these practices of mindless consumption of ideas and compliance to enforced standards that may be informed by outdated policies that seek to maintain the status quo, and instead engage actively in practices that place teachers in the driver's seat.

The latter lets them spawn revolutions within classroom spaces that have the potential to impact the larger society in significant ways. In this way, we nurture future educators who are thinkers and not blind followers of rules! Giroux (2016) remarks further:

> For the most part, public school teachers and higher education faculty are a national treasure and may be one of the last defenses undermining a growing authoritarianism and pervasive racism, permanent war culture, widening inequality and debased notions of citizenship in US society. They can't solve these problems but they can educate a generation of students to address them. (n.p.)

A critical approach to teaching lends itself well to this social justice enterprise; of course, nonfiction literature is always also a good place to engage in such practices.

At this point, it is necessary to reiterate the notion of nonfiction encompassing much more than social history as well as appearing in multiple forms, as the discussion in the next section demonstrates. And as Griffith (2017) rightly observes, this kind of storytelling is "saddled with many genre labels" (p. 4), some of which include creative, literary, and narrative nonfiction.

It is also considered a how-to genre for those who would simply like to know how to perform a task—fix something, cook something, plant something, self-development, and, to be consistent with a strand in this book, become an activist. It is important that educators convey the significance and dynamism of this genre to students.

GEORGE MCGAVIN'S *BUGS: A STUNNING POP-UP LOOK AT INSECTS, SPIDERS, AND OTHER CREEPY-CRAWLIES*

Switching from conversations on social history with a particular focus on transatlantic slavery to conversations on natural history with a focus on bugs affords readers a chance for another kind of critical dialogue, and exposure to one more kind of nonfiction—texts that engage the natural environment.

I may start by saying that I do not really care for bugs. They cause me anxiety; however, having grown up at an oil palm plantation owned by the former British Unilever Corporation, where entomology played a significant part in how company officials managed the plants, crops, and the environment, I got accustomed to bugs. I also understood their relevance to the survival and/or destruction of palm produce, the lifeline of the natives and inhabitants of that region of the African continent, and to the ecosystem.

McGavin's nonfiction book is about bugs. A renowned British entomologist whose research has taken him all over the globe, McGavin (2014) asserts that,

> Insects have endured for hundreds of millions of years. They have survived the numerous global upheavals and catastrophes that spelled the end for much greater and grander creatures and they will continue to be a major part of the Earth's fauna for many more millennia. (n.p.)

This is a compelling case for writing a nonfiction book on insects for young readers. His pop-up book, illustrated by Jim Kay, opens with him telling readers about the different "kinds of bugs (or arthropods, to give them their scientific name)" (unpaged). He identifies the types accompanied by illustrations and/or lifelike images of these bugs, which children can actually explore.

The organization of the book reflects what one may speculate are his objectives for writing this book: "So Many Different Bugs," "How Bugs Work," "The Life of a Bug," "Why the World Needs Bugs," "Where Bugs Live," and "My Ultimate Bugs."

His point of view and subjectivities as an entomologist are ever-present and are made visible in his use of language. For instance, in the section "My Ultimate Bugs," he shares a list that ranges from the "deadliest fat-tailed scorpion" to the "seventeen-year cicada," but it is not clear why these are his favorites. There are nine in total.

The rhetorical strategy that shapes the narrative serves his purpose here, since he opened with his "many travels around the world that opportune him to encounter different kinds of bugs" (unpaged). It is understandable that he may have favorites. This, however, does not necessarily imply that these are every entomologist's favorite.

Critical readers sense his subjectivity immediately in his selection, for these may not be their favorite too. Therefore, while the facts about each bug may be accurate, the sentiments may differ. He is passionate about some bugs but we do not know why, and so this is a subjective stance that may signal some kind of red flag to the reader.

The engineering behind the construction of the book itself makes for a critical discussion that can lead students to create their own pop-up books on any subject. It also affords students possibilities for more inquiry about (1) the book-making process and (2) our natural world—what they would like to know that might not have been of interest to the author of this particular book. Spectacular to look at, grab, trace, explore, read, and play with, McGavin and Kay's (2014) nonfiction book offers several occasions for readers to ponder the "truths" narrated about arthropods.

Resources online on insects call for identification activities and as such recommend the efferent reading stance: taking away information from the text (Rosenblatt, 1995). However, looking at bugs, the conversation could go beyond simply regurgitating important information about the insects and instances of literary devices that may stand as evidence that the book is nonfiction.

Focusing on the point of view, the multimodal and other linguistic aspects of the narratives from a critical stance can lead readers to pose thoughtful questions about arthropods in general, such as, what are their value to human beings? How do they contribute to the protection of the environment? How do they help to maintain the lifecycle of the ecosystem? Researching other sources also expands readers' knowledge on these topics.

In all three examples of nonfiction books discussed here (Granfield, Aronson and Budho, and McGavin), there is always a basic need to engage the narrative at the personal, emotional, and intellectual levels, research multiple sources for accuracy of facts, and debate the issues that are presented by authors from their unique perspectives. This approach is consistent with Aronson's advice that knowledge should not simply be received, but should be pursued (http://www.marcaronson.com/professor/).

This is an idea that educators could translate into their daily practice, as we encourage readers to participate in conversations about our physical, natural, and socio-historical worlds with expectations that they would also take an interest in crafting their own "truths," as Griffith's tenth graders did about a particular event to illustrate truth relativity (2017, p. 66). This is a major objective of this volume, and the ensuing chapters offer various perspectives on how this is being done or can occur in classroom settings in public schools and colleges.

With the understanding that teachers often turn to award-winning books to make decisions on what texts to include in their curriculum, the next section introduces four award-winning authors whose works elevated the status of nonfiction children's literature within the discipline, one for being the first nonfiction book to ever win a Newbery Medal (Henrik Van Loon); the second (Russell Freedman), for winning books across the three major award categories; the third (Jean Fritz), for winning the first Orbis Pictus award for Outstanding Nonfiction for Children; and the fourth (Marc Aronson), for winning the first Robert I. Sibert International Book Medal.

AWARD-WINNING AUTHORS

Several authors of fine nonfiction have won awards. However, this section showcases four only. Some of the authors (Van Loon, Freedman, Fritz, and Aronson) highlighted in this section have since won more awards for the quality of their nonfiction, with Freedman winning a medal in each of the three categories (1988 Newbery Medal, 1995 Orbis Pictus Award, and 2005 Sibert Medal), and receiving a Newbery honor for three other titles, *The Voice That Changed a Nation: Marian Anderson and the Struggle for Equal*

Rights (2005 honor book), *Eleanor Roosevelt: A Life of Discovery* (1994 honor book), and *The Wright Brothers: How They Invented the Airplane* (1992 honor book).

Knickerbocker, Brueggeman, and Rycik (2012) assert that Russell Freedman's *Lincoln: A Photobiography*, published in 1987 and which earned a Newbery Medal,

> covers the entirety of Lincoln's life from his backwoods beginnings to his assassination, in approximately 130 pages of texts and pictures. . . . Freedman presents a multifaceted man, a man who was at times plagued with depression, emotionally distant, lacking in military acumen, and superstitious. He was also brilliant, ambitious, and determined to keep the country intact. (p. 240)

In a scholastic interview transcript, Freedman reiterates the point of the author making decisions about what to include or leave out. His insistence on the power the author has in the creative process alerts readers even more about the need for a critical lens when navigating texts with facts that employ narrative devices that touch us emotionally and make us think about the person or subject in distinct ways.

In an interview for the Horn Book (Sutton, 2002) where Freedman explains his process in some detail, he reminds readers of our subjectivities, asserting that,

> Let's say history is what happened. The *record* of what happened is how each individual happens to see those events. They've already been filtered . . . it's impossible to write about anyone, any event, in any period of time, without in some way imposing, even unconsciously, your own standards, your own values. (n.p.)

If it is that "impossible," educators should make a concerted effort to equip students with critical thinking skills that afford them the academic and creative tools to investigate, interrogate, and rethink/rewrite/re-create nonfiction texts, including those that explore scientific and mathematical truths. Such re-creations can be based on factual accounts but utilize rhetorical devices and/or storytelling strategies that add a personal touch and as such center each student's perspective.

In this way, students are also able to leave their marks as truth makers from their truth-seeking investigative experience. This expectation is not limited only to literary and narrative nonfiction based on history. It can also be applied to other kinds of expository and creative nonfiction texts, and on other subjects such as science. Below is a table of some award-winning books and trailblazing authors in nonfiction.

In the chapters that follow, contributors share how conversations unfold or might unfold around social issues in nonfiction texts with particular foci

Table 1.1. Authors Who Won the First Nonfiction Book in Each Category or Awards in All Three Major Categories of Interest.

Author	Award	Book Title	Year
Hendrick Willem van Loon	The Newbery Medal	*The Story of Mankind*	1922
Russell Freedman	The Newbery Medal	*Lincoln: A Photobiography*	1988
	Orbis Pictus Award	*Children of the Great Depression*	2006
	Robert Sibert Award	*The Voice That Challenged the Nation*	2005
Jean Fritz	Orbis Pictus Award	*The Great Little Madison*	1990
Marc Aronson	Robert F. Sibert Award	*Sir Walter Raleigh and the Quest for El Dorado*	2001

on politics, religion, social history, and life in general at educational and other settings. They discuss their critical inquiries on pertinent issues, explaining in some detail how learners—child and adult—are responding or have responded to issues of social justice encountered in texts.

This also is in an attempt to encourage newcomers into the profession to consider critical inquiry as a vehicle through which they might come to understand how learners think about issues literacy educators hold dear. Following such inquiries are informed pedagogical practices. Teacher candidates fall into this category of "young" professionals.

As the child advocates that they are expected to be, and to become, more so once they graduate and in their own classrooms, it is vital that teacher candidates, too, continue to cultivate a mind-set of possibility, and of investigation that would predispose them to creative thinking and risk-taking adventures in their chosen career paths.

In addition, decolonial theorist De Lissovoy (2010) reminds us that,

> Students and teachers have to understand the fact of political conquest, and the process of cultural and epistemological assimilation corresponding to it, and participate in the unraveling of these processes, if they are to be involved in a truly democratic form of education. (p. 290)

Nurturing curious learners who participate in knowledge production is therefore strongly encouraged.

And yes, the world is full of people eager to learn—using nonfiction literature in a transdisciplinary and/or transformative manner, we are all encouraged to ask "why?" and to ponder "what if?" opening the floodgates to endless opportunities for exploration, and the kinds of adventure to which Aronson succinctly refers. This will unfold organically with an educator—

mediating learners' experiences that allow for creativity and inquiry within a flexible structure. We should not be silenced by the formidable system that forever resists change, or by knowledge brokers who insist on only one way of knowing and seeing! Interrogating representations of social issues is just one path on this journey to self-actualization.

REFERENCES

Aronson, M. CiSSL Talks—Non-fiction and the Common Core Standards. Retrieved from http://www.marcaronson.com/professor/.

Aronson, M., & Budhos, M. (2010). *Sugar Changed the World: A Story of Magic, Spice, Slavery, Freedom, and Science*. New York, NY: Clarion Books.

Brummel, B. (Producer). (1998). *Ku Klux Klan: A Secret History*. New York: New Video Group.

Collier, L. (2016). No Longer Invisible: How Diverse Children's Literature Helps Children Find Themselves in Books and Why It Matters. *The Council Chronicle* (pp. 13–17). Retrieved from http://www.ncte.org/library/NCTEFiles/Resources/Journals/CC/0261-sept 2016/NoLongerInvisible.pdf.

De Lissovoy. (2010). Decolonial Pedagogy and the Ethics of the Global. *Discourse: Studies in the Cultural Politics of Education* 31, no. 3: 279–93.

Freedman, R. (n.d). Author Interviews: Russell Freedman Interview Transcript. Retrieved from http://www.scholastic.com/teachers/article/russell-freedman-interview-transcript.

Giroux, H. (2016). Why Teachers Matter in Dark Times. *Truthout*. Retrieved from http://www.truth-out.org/opinion/item/35970-why-teachers-matter-in-dark-times.

Goodreads. Retrieved from http://www.goodreads.com/book/show/434472.Sugar_Changed_the_World.

Granfield, L. (2009). *Out of Slavery: The Journey to Amazing Grace*. Illustrated by Janet Wilson. Canada: Tundra Books.

———. (1997). *Amazing Grace: The Story of the Hymn*. Illustrated by Janet Wilson. Canada: Tundra Books.

Griffith, J. (2017). *From Me to We: Using Narrative Nonfiction to Broaden Student Perspectives*. New York: Routledge Education.

Knickerbocker, J., Brueggeman, M., & Rycik, J. (2012). *Literature for Young Adults: Books and More for Contemporary Readers*. Scottsdale, AZ: Holcomb Hathaway Publishers.

McGavin, G. (2014). Why I Love . . . Insects. Retrieved from https://www.theguardian.com/lifeandstyle/2014/sep/26/why-i-love-insects.

McGavin, G. (2013). *Bugs: A Stunning Pop-Up Look at Insects, Spiders, and Other Creepy-Crawlies*. Somerville, MA: Candlewick.

Rosenblatt, L. M. (1995). *Literature as Exploration*. New York, NY: The Modern Language Association.

Sutton, R. (2002). An Interview with Russell Freedman. *The Horn Book*. Retrieved from http://www.hbook.com/2002/11/authors-illustrators/interviews/interview-russell-freedman/#.

Transcript from an Interview with Marc Aronson: Evidence and Nuance in Nonfiction Texts. Retrieved from http://www.readingrockets.org/books/interviews/aronson/transcript.

Zarnowski, M., Kerper, R., & Jensen, J. (2001) (Eds.). *The Best in Nonfiction: Reading, Writing and Teaching Orbis Pictus Award Winning Books*. Urbana, IL: National Council of Teachers of English.

Yenika-Agbaw, V. (2006). Capitalism and the Culture of Hate in Granfield's *Amazing Grace: The Story of the Hymn. Journal of Black Studies* 36, no. 3: 253–61.

Chapter Two

You, Too, Can Make a Difference

Young Civil Rights Activists

Terrell A. Young, Barbara A. Ward, and Deanna Day

> Making history is not just the activity of a few heroic people. It's mass moments of ordinary people building up enough steam to do something about it.
> —Russell Freedman (in Lehman, 2007)

The Declaration of Independence proclaims that "all men are created equal" and thus entitled to such rights as "life, liberty, and the pursuit of happiness." Yet various groups, including workers, women, people of color, and American Indians, fought, and continue to fight, for those rights that are freely available to white Americans. The term "civil rights" is typically associated with the personal liberties of the citizens of a country, including freedom of speech and protection from certain types of discrimination. In 1964, Congress passed the Civil Rights Act, ending segregation and banning all discrimination based on color, race, religion, or national origin.

While the civil rights movement is considered one of the most celebrated events in American history, surprisingly, it receives little attention in most US classrooms (Damon, 2012; Southern Poverty Law Center, 2011). Often, teachers and students seem to think that the battle for civil rights ended decades ago and has little relevance in the twenty-first century.

However, Allie, a preservice teacher in one of our classes, noted, "I used to think that civil rights issues were no longer relevant, but then while I was reading Susan Goldman Rubin's *Freedom Summer: The 1964 Struggle for Civil Rights in Mississippi* (2014), I heard about the shootings in a church in Charleston. I realized that our country has a lot of work to guarantee those rights to all Americans." Not all of our future teachers have had that realization.

Reading and discussing civil rights forces "students to grapple with issues of oppression and democracy in US society" (Bettis, Cooks, & Bergin, 1994, p. 209) and has many benefits for students:

1. "Students can easily recognize the goals, struggles, and social conflicts that defined the major events";
2. "Students can learn about universal values of human rights and social justice in the context of the particulars of U.S. citizenship";
3. Students develop a sense of "hope that their efforts can achieve results and belief that their society is worth their efforts and their sacrifices" through reading of successful stories of the movement (Damon, 2012, p. 25–26).

Often "readers who are naïve, narrow minded, or prejudiced" can have their "heads and hearts softened" by reading and discussing compelling nonfiction about the civil rights movement (Crowe, 2003, p. 132).

Dylan was such a student. He chose to read *They Called Themselves the K.K.K.: The Birth of an American Terrorist Group* (Bartoletti, 2012) for a literature circle group. "I could only read one chapter per day because of the way blacks were treated and how the Klan literally got away with murder," he said. "Then when I learned that the K.K.K. is still active in some parts of our country I just felt sick. I realized that I *needed* to read this book."

Experts in children's literature agree with him, arguing that ignoring challenging topics is a mistake.

> While we might wish that children did not have to deal with issues like racism, poverty, and war, the fact of the matter is that many children are deeply concerned about these difficult issues when they walk into our classrooms. Ignoring what they need help to understand and deal with is not productive or humane. (Leland, Harste, & Huber, 2015, p. 98)

Because familiarity with civil rights is one of the hallmarks of a democracy and young people can play an important part in preserving those rights for themselves and others, this chapter focuses on children's and young adults' contributions to the civil rights movement.

In the remainder of the chapter, we examine the role of historical nonfiction in teaching and learning history, strategies teachers can use to explore and respond to historical nonfiction to teach about the civil rights, and include excerpts from an interview with award-winning author Larry Dane Brimner, who is well known for his excellent historical books about the civil rights movement.

HISTORICAL NONFICTION

Historical nonfiction serves an important role in helping students make sense of many aspects of history (Zarnowski, 2006). This is certainly true of the civil rights movement. Learning how others suffered because of Jim Crow laws brings the period to life for today's students. Gardener notes that "autobiographical accounts allow students to gain an appreciation for the struggles, hardships, victories, defeats, possibilities, and limitations of civil rights on an intimate level" (2002, p. 98).

According to Zarnowski (2006), such literature has two main roles: (1) "providing background information in a clear and engaging way," and (2) showing students "how to think about history" (p. 29). Moreover, *We've Got a Job* (Levinson, 2012) is an excellent example of a book about the civil rights movement that builds students' background knowledge in a clear and engaging manner. Levinson weaves together the stories of four children who were involved in the Birmingham Children's March against segregation.

Zarnowski (2006) explains how authors of historical nonfiction literature show students how to think about history in the following manner:

> They address issues such as lack of evidence, contradictory evidence, multiple interpretations of the same events, and the relevance of the past to the present as these issues arise in their own work. Instead of brushing these thought-provoking issues under the carpet, authors of historical nonfiction highlight them for a young audience, they do not assume students know how to read history or critique what they read at a sophisticated level. They provide a helping hand. (pp. 33–34)

In *Claudette Colvin: Twice Towards Justice* (2009), Phillip Hoose provides contradictory evidence to a commonly known civil rights narrative. Most students have learned about Rosa Parks refusing to give up her seat on a crowded Montgomery bus, but few are familiar with Claudette Colvin's story. Only nine months before the Rosa Parks incident, fifteen-year-old Claudette was unwilling to allow a white woman to take her bus seat.

Instead of being celebrated like Rosa Parks, Colvin was shunned, dismissed, nearly forgotten, and sacrificed for the good of the larger cause. Hoose helps readers question whose stories are included and whose are omitted from history.

When students do become interested in the civil rights movement, they often react with shame and guilt, almost paralyzed into inaction and frustration. For example, after reading the March trilogy (Lewis & Aydin, 2013, 2015, 2016), Abigail, a preservice teacher, expressed her disappointment in her own education about civil rights. "None of my classes ever discussed this back in elementary or high school," she said, "and I feel kind of embarrassed about that and what I don't know. I can't believe I had to learn about civil rights and Freedom Summer from a graphic novel intended for young readers."

Another classmate, Emily, echoed her comments, but then turned the discussion in a different direction. "Yes, I feel sheepish, and concerned about what I didn't learn. But most of all, what I'm feeling now is this pressure to do something about my feelings. What do I do now? How can I make a difference? After all, I'm just one person and just one teacher."

Larry Dane Brimner, author of several civil rights–related books, including *Birmingham Sunday* (2010), *Black & White: The Confrontation between Rev. Fred L. Shuttlesworth and Eugene (Bull) Connor* (2011), *We Are One: The Story of Bayard Rustin* (2007), and *12 Days in May: Freedom Ride 1961* (2017), understands those feelings of guilt and helplessness, but suggests that change begins at home with each individual. He urges students "not to become isolated, but rather to be open to new cultural experiences, to venture into the unfamiliar" (personal communication, June 29, 2017).

While marching in protests and speaking out against unfair practices are important, Brimner suggests that simple but effective changes can sometimes occur when individuals "look within their own hearts and ask how they would like to be treated, and then treat everyone in that way" (personal communication, June 29, 2017).

No matter the age level, readers can draw inspiration from the examples of young people who dared to make a difference, either by taking an individual stand or aligning themselves with others in a group. For instance, *Child of the Civil Rights Movement* (Shelton, 2009) relates the early experiences and insider perspective of Paula, daughter of Andrew Young, one of the early civil rights leaders.

In *Turning 15 on the Road to Freedom: My Story of the 1965 Selma Voting Rights March* (Lowery, 2015), readers are taken to the front lines of the march for suffrage and the multiple attempts to cross that bridge in Selma, Alabama. Over and over, children and teens are seen as having important roles in a political movement and are themselves regarded as political activists.

This is particularly evident in *We've Got a Job: The 1963 Birmingham Children's March* (Levinson, 2012) in which schoolchildren stayed home from their classes in order to march for civil rights and force the hands of legal authorities in their city, causing the city's jails to overflow with young prisoners and, some say, breathing new life into the civil rights movement.

EXPLORING CIVIL RIGHTS AND RACE

There is no chart, formula, or script providing a blueprint on effectively engaging students in discussions about civil rights. But children's and young adult literature provide rich contexts for beginning and sustaining conversations on this topic with its roots in history and branches in the future.

Children's literature validates experiences for some children and raises issues for other children. One beginning point might be to have students consider whether their teachers have made the fight for civil rights visible or whether there are class discussions related to race.

Teachers themselves might benefit from reflecting on how or whether they discuss these issues with their students. Asking themselves about how comfortable they feel about raising issues around race in their own classrooms might provide insight into their own reluctance to address difficult questions and explore tough issues. While many teachers claim to be color blind and see all their students the same way, race and ethnicity are arguably essential elements of each person's identity.

Selecting authentic nonfiction books about civil rights for classrooms can make cultures, languages, history, class, gender, race, age, and disability more visible to students. Children's literature invites conversations around social issues and helps students question why racism still exists today. It also enriches students' understanding by giving voice to those who have been silenced (Ociepka & Vasquez, 2000).

Ideally, teachers should choose texts where children's voices tell the story, not an adult. Selecting quality books may even move students to take some kind of action (Short, 2012). Copenhaver-Johnson (2007) suggests that teachers must first create a safe classroom environment in order to foster a space to talk about race. Selecting quality picture books to read aloud that discuss race, and then inviting students to respond during the reading versus waiting until the end when it seems rushed, helps students talk about difficult topics.

Copenhaver-Johnson (2007) further suggests that during the read-aloud, teachers demonstrate their own wondering talk, sharing their uncertainties with statements such as "I wonder," "What if," "Have you ever," "I don't agree, and "I have experienced something different"; this helps students see that teachers are willing to search alongside them to find answers to questions and concerns. In addition, during discussions on race, children should talk to one another. Strict rules of raising hands signals to children that they have to talk to the teacher only. Student-to-student dialogue will empower them to have conversations about critical issues.

Critically reading or getting to "why" racial tension exists in the twenty-first century may help students think about changes (Freire, 1997). Critical literacy practices encourage students to use language to question our world, to interrogate the relationships between language and power, to analyze popular culture and media, to understand how power relationships are socially constructed, and to consider actions that can be taken to promote social justice (Lewison, Lewis, & Harste, 2008).

Through the use of children's literature, teachers can help readers become active participants in the reading process where they move beyond passively accepting a text's message to question, examine, or dispute the power relationships between readers and authors. Critical literacy focuses on the issues of power and promotes reflection, transformation, and action (McLaughlin & DeVoogd, 2004). For example, Dutro, Kazemi, and Balf (2005) suggest these questions to help students think about texts (see Figure 2.1).

Matching nonfiction text with a fiction title sometimes helps students gain a larger perspective on the civil rights movement. Nonfiction may be difficult for students to understand, so pairing with fiction could be beneficial. For example, it can be effective to pair picture books such as *Freedom Summer* (Wiles, 2005), *Sister Ann's Hands* (Loribecki, 2000), and *The Other Side* (Woodson, 2001) with nonfiction titles such as *A Wreath for Emmett Till* (Nelson, 2006) and *Freedom Riders: John Lewis and Jim Zwerg on the Front Lines of the Civil Rights Movement* (Bausum, 2006), or *12 Days in May: Freedom Ride 1961* (Brimner, 2017).

Another useful teaching idea involves organizing a text set of books around the theme of race or the civil rights movement from the list of books at the close of this chapter. Text sets are simply single copies of books on a theme, issue, topic, or author. Hade (1997) notes that the content of picture books may appear to be simple and reassuring when they are read by themselves, but they can become problematized in the company of a book that takes a different perspective.

Having students read as many of the books in the text set as they can might take over a week or longer while taking notes deepens their understanding of a topic or issue. If they then discuss the books in a literature circle, comparing and contrasting different approaches to the topic, students may gain a larger perspective on civil rights.

Who benefits (from this text, practice, situation)?
In whose interest (is this written, is this policy made, was that statement made)?
What was the purpose (of the text, practice, policy, statement)?
How would someone else (or a different character) have experienced this differently?
What beliefs (or values or assumptions) about race lie behind that statement (or action)?
What would you have done differently?
Have you ever experienced something like this?
Why haven't you (or why have you)?
What language do we use to talk about these issues?
Where do those terms come from?

Figure 2.1. Critical Literacy Questions from Dutro, Kazemi, and Balf (2005).

Reading or hearing a story one time often is not enough. Lingering with a story or book helps students of all ages discover new insights and gives them a chance to see things differently. Lingering also helps expand other participants' understandings. In the elementary grades, lingering is typically reading a book three times over three consecutive days (Leland, Lewison, & Harste, 2013).

Lingering over books could occur in the form of various discussions during which students discuss personal connections they made to the text in a small group after their first reading. Then after the second reading, students ask questions about the text of their group members. They try to answer the questions too. Finally, after the third reading, the small groups discuss how this text connects to larger issues within the community or culture.

Leland, Lewison, and Harste (2013) suggest students present their thoughts/feelings through alternate sign systems besides writing or language arts. Along with Short, Kauffman, and Kahn (2000), these authors explain that using sign systems challenges readers (or listeners) to articulate the underlying meaning of stories. For example, using *Claudette Colvin: Twice toward Justice* (Hoose, 2009), a teacher could read aloud the first chapter entitled "Jim Crow and the Detested Number Ten." As students listen to the chapter, they can use watercolor paints to create a response to the chapter. Students then share their paintings, comparing and contrasting their responses.

The next day the teacher could read aloud chapter 2, entitled "Coot." Students could use math manipulatives such as Unifix Cubes, blocks, or tangrams to create responses or respond artistically to the chapter after the read-aloud through artwork, an interpretive dance, a song, found poetry, or even a dramatic monologue that would be shared with their classmates. Students could complete a museum walk and look at their classmates' different artistic interpretations of the chapter.

On the third day, the teacher reads aloud chapter 3, "We Seemed to Hate Ourselves." After the read-aloud, small groups of four or five students could be formed, with each student choosing a character to play, with the group deciding on a tableau or frozen picture that shows their understanding or retelling of the entire story so far (see Figure 2.2 for tableaux directions). This process could be continued, and other sign systems used to respond to the text. Closing the read-aloud with a discussion on how the meaning of the story was expanded or constrained through the transmediation and sign system process validates the experience.

Teachers can use biography breaks to introduce students to the historical context and people who played a role in the civil rights movement. Biography breaks involve the teacher reading aloud a picture book biography and engaging students in a brief discussion (Young & Miner, 2015). Heisey and Kucan (2010) suggest that teachers ask one or two questions while reading to

- Find two other people to work with. As a group decide on a civil rights book that you all like and take turns reading it aloud.
- While reading pay special attention to what the characters are doing and thinking.
- After reading, discuss what you all think are the most important issues in the book.
- Everyone picks a character to play and together decide on a tableau (frozen picture) that shows your group's understanding of the story. Your tableau might not be an actual scene from the book.
- Create a tableau:
  Who are we (characters, roles)
  Where are we (setting, context)
  What are we doing (problem, tension)
  Why are we doing it? (focus, theme, issue)
  How will we show this? (body language, movement, mood)
- You probably want to try out a number of tableaux before you find one that captures your ideas the best.
- Make name tags for your characters to wear.
- Perform your tableau in front of the class. Hold perfectly still for a minute and then have each character say one line that sums up who he or she is and what he or she is feeling.
- Teacher debriefs with students after the presentations--How did you feel playing that role? Was it difficult? What did you learn about your character?

Figure 2.2. Tableau Directions (Hertzberg, 2003).

focus students' attention on important content. Sometimes, students will then ask questions that can later become the subject of their personal or small group inquiries (Young & Miner, 2015).

A biography break based on Jabari Asim's (2016) *Preaching to the Chickens: The Story of Young John Lewis* will provide students with a fascinating story of the childhood of Congressman John Lewis, one of the original Freedom Riders and an award-winning author. Cynthia Levinson's (2017) *The Youngest Marcher: The Story of Audrey Faye Hendricks, a Young Civil Rights Activist* will introduce students to the youngest child who was involved in the Birmingham Children's March—one of four thousand who missed school to protest segregation and one of twenty-five hundred who was jailed at age nine for her protest.

Biography breaks about school desegregation might include Robert Cole's (1995) *The Ruby Bridges Story* and Duncan Tonatiuh's (2014) *Separate Is Never Equal: Sylvia Mendez and Her Family's Fight for Desegregation*.

CONCLUSION

Au (1990) suggests that teachers who adopt transformation and social action approaches in their classrooms show a deep commitment to literacy learning and citizenship of all students. Using culturally conscious literature enables students to explore social issues in a thoughtful, positive manner. Through a social action approach, they help students to understand the responsibility every citizen should feel for the fair treatment and well-being of all groups within the United States.

It is important, even in 2017, more than five decades after the passage of the Civil Rights Act, to examine current instructional practices. Teachers will want to consider the types of reading materials and approaches they are using in their classrooms. Teachers must take inventory of their current practices and the books they choose to share with their students.

It might be helpful to explore whether their selected trade books are titles that offer students hope and empower them. It is essential to provide time for discussion and writing about how to make this a better world by sharing children's or adolescent books. Teachers must also take care to teach their students the skills they will need to critically think about issues and then take social action.

Ultimately, teachers will be impressed to learn that there is a plethora of resources on civil rights and social justice, even finding excellent lesson plans and activities on websites such as teachingtolerance.org or from book lists such as those announced annually by the Notable Books for a Global Society.

So many of the stories of civil rights, from those of the very first legal efforts to thwart segregation in schools back in the 1850s as described in *The First Step* (Rubin, 2016), on through *Separate Is Never Equal* (Tonatiuh, 2014), attest to the importance of youth in causing social changes.

The stories of those who came before them may inspire the current generation to their own words and deeds. "Personal narratives, in other words, help make real the pains and passions that not only shaped ordinary people's experiences, but also led many into activism. In the end, personal narratives provide students with the messiness of history by offering them alternative and often competing versions of struggles for freedom" (Gardener, 2002, p. 98).

REFERENCES

Au, K.H. (1998). Social constructivism and the school literacy learning of students of diverse backgrounds. *Journal of Literacy Research, 30*(2), 297–319.

Bettis, P.J., Cooks, H.C., and Bergin, D.A. (1994). "It's not steps anymore, but more like shuffling": Students' perceptions of the civil rights movement and ethnic identity. *The Journal of Negro Education, 63*(2), 197–211.

Copenhaver-Johnson, J.F., Bowman, J.T., and Johnson, A.C. (2007). Santa stories: Children's inquiry about race during picturebook read-alouds. *Language Arts, 84*(3), 234–44.
Crowe, C. (2003). Reading African American history and the civil rights movement. *English Journal, 92*(3), 131–34.
Damon, W. (2012). Failing liberty 101. *Educational Leadership, 69*(7), 22–26.
Dutro, E., Kazemi, E., and Balf, R. (2005). The aftermath of "You're only half": Multiracial identities in the literacy classroom. *Language Arts, 83*(2), 96.
Freire, P. (1997). *Pedagogy of the heart*. New York, NY: Continuum.
Gardener, S.E. (2002). Coming of age in the movement: Teaching with personal narratives. In J.B. Armstrong, S.H. Edwards, H.B. Roberson, and R.Y. Williams (Eds.), *Teaching the American Civil Rights Movement: Freedom's bittersweet song* (pp. 97–110). New York, NY: Routledge.
Hade, D. (1997). Reading multiculturally. In T. Rogers and A. Soter (Eds.), *Reading across cultures: Teaching literature in a diverse society* (pp. 233–55). New York: Teachers College Press.
Heisey, N., and Kucan, L. (2010). Introducing science concepts to primary students through read alouds: Interactions and multiple texts make a difference. *The Reading Teacher, 63*, 666–76.
Hertzberg, M. (2003). Engaging critical reader response to literature through process drama. *Reading Online, 6*(10). Retrieved from http://www.readingonline.org/international/hertzberg/.
Lehman, C. (2007). Telling the story in history: An interview with Russell Freedman. Retrieved from http://www.cybils.com/2007/03/telling_the_sto.html.
Leland, C., Lewison, M., and Harste, J. (2013). *Teaching children's literature: It's critical*. New York, NY: Routledge.
Leland, C.H., Harste, J.C., and Huber, K.R. (2015). Critical literacy in a first-grade classroom. In K. Winograd (Ed.), *Critical literacies and young learners: Connecting classroom practice to the Common Core* (pp. 86–101). New York, NY: Routledge.
Short, K.G. (2012). Children's agency for taking action. *Bluebird, 50*(4), 41–50.
Short, K.G., Kauffman, G., and Kahn, L.H. (2000). "I just need to draw": Responding to literature across multiple sign systems. *The Reading Teacher, 54*, 160–71.
Southern Poverty Law Center. (2011). *Teaching the movement: The state of civil rights education in the United States 2011*. Montgomery, AL: Author.
Young, T.A., and Miner, A.B. (2015). Guiding inquiry with biography breaks and the C3 framework: Can one person make a difference? *The Reading Teacher, 69*(3), 311–19.
Zarnowski, M. (2006). *Making sense of history: Using high-quality literature and hands-on experiences to build content knowledge*. New York, NY: Scholastic.

CHILDREN'S AND YOUNG ADULT CIVIL RIGHTS BOOKS

Asim, J. (2016). *Preaching to the chickens: The story of young John Lewis*. Illustrated by E.B. Lewis. New York, NY: Nancy Paulsen Books.
Bausum, A. (2006). *Freedom Riders: John Lewis and Jim Zwerg on the front lines of the Civil Rights movement*. Washington, DC: National Geographic.
Bolden, T. (2007). *M.L.K.: Journey of a king*. New York, NY: Abrams.
Brimner, L.D. (2010). *Birmingham Sunday*. Honesdale, PA: Calkins Creek.
Brimner, L.D. (2011). *Black & white: The confrontation between Reverend Fred L. Shuttlesworth and Eugene "Bull" Connor*. Honesdale, PA: Calkins Creek.
Brimner, L.D. (2014). *STRIKE! The farmworkers fight for their rights*. Honesdale, PA: Calkins Creek.
Brimner, L.D. (2017). *12 days in May: Freedom Ride 1961*. Honesdale, PA: Calkins Creek.
Hoose, P. (2009). *Claudette Colvin: Twice towards justice*. New York, NY: Farrar, Straus and Giroux.

Levine, E. (2000). *Freedom's children: Young civil rights activists tell their own stories.* New York, NY: Penguin.

Levinson, C. (2012). *We've got a job: The 1963 Birmingham children's march.* Atlanta, GA: Peachtree.

Levinson, C. (2017). *The youngest marcher: The Story of Audrey Faye Hendricks, a young civil rights activist.* Illustrated by V. Brantley-Newton. New York, NY: Atheneum.

Lewis, J., and Aydin, A. (2013). *March: Book One.* Illustrated by N. Powell. Marietta, GA: Top Shelf Productions.

Lewis, J., and Aydin, A. (2015). *March: Book Two.* Illustrated by N. Powell. Marietta, GA: Top Shelf Productions.

Lewis, J., and Aydin, A. (2016). *March: Book Three.* Illustrated by N. Powell. Marietta, GA: Top Shelf Productions.

Lorbiecki, M. (2000). *Sister Anne's hands.* Illustrated by W. Popp. New York, NY: Puffin Books.

Lowery, L.B. (2015). *Turning 15 on the road to freedom: My story of the 1965 Selma Voting Rights March.* New York, NY: Dial.

Rubin, S.G. (2016). *The first step: How one girl put segregation on trial.* Illustrated by E.B. Lewis. New York, NY: Bloomsbury.

Rubin, S.G. (2014). *Freedom summer: The 1964 struggle for civil rights in Mississippi.* New York, NY: Holiday House.

Shelton, P.Y. (2009). *Child of the Civil Rights movement.* New York, NY: Schwartz & Wade.

Tonatiuh, D. (2014). *Separate is never equal: Sylvia Mendez and her family's fight for desegregation.* New York, NY: Harry N. Abrams.

Wiles, D. (2005). *Freedom summer.* Illustrated by J. Lagarrique. New York, NY: Aladdin.

Woodson, J. (2001). *The other side.* Illustrated by E.B. Lewis. New York, NY: G.P. Putnam's Sons Books.

Chapter Three

Advocating for Immigrant Experiences in Nonfiction Literature

Ruth McKoy Lowery, Kathleen Colantonio-Yurko, and Cody Miller

> In a peaceful world without the threat of global warming or conflict or war, where everyone has access to education, health care, food and a dignified life, there would still be a need for critical literacy. In a world that is rich with difference, there is still likely to be intolerance and fear of the other. Because difference is structured in relation to power, unequal access to resources based on gender, race, ethnicity, language, ability, sexuality, nationality and class will continue to produce privilege and resentment. Even in a world where socially constructed relations of power have been flattened, we will still have to manage the politics of our daily lives.
> —Janks, 2012, p. 150

Eighteen years ago, the twenty-first century was ushered in with conversations about global citizenship, equity and diversity, social justice education, and caring and empathy for others who differ culturally, ethnically, and demographically from mainstream American citizens (Banks, 2006; Lowery, 2000). Although these conversations continue to dominate the research, particularly in critical discussions about representations in literature for children and young adults, still inequity in the storying abounds.

Differences of language and power seem to be inevitably intertwined in our increasingly diverse country, but the prevalent images of diverse groups portrayed across various social media platforms continue to offer a negative narrative that still demands to be queried through critical lenses. The suppression of Native Americans, African Americans, Asian Americans, and other culturally and linguistically diverse groups is a sad and unfortunate part of American history that still exists, but advocates continue to push for an educational experience that helps students to learn about and experience the rich cultures that exist outside their lived realities (Alsup & Miller, 2014).

The belief that some people's experiences are more valued in American society and thus everyone should conform to one ideal presents a counternarrative, and the push for others to be included in the conversation continues to permeate literary discussions (Al-Hazza, 2010; Short, 2011). The argument for integrating literature about immigrant and global experiences in schools' curricula becomes more important, and, one might argue, more urgent, as negative sentiments surrounding immigrants in the United States become more vitriolic.

For instance, a survey regarding the effects of the 2016 presidential election on kindergarten to twelfth-grade students conducted by the Southern Poverty Law Center found that one-third of teachers reported an increase in anti-immigrant sentiments as a result of the election (Costello, 2016). Lowery (2000) agrees that traditionally negative values, beliefs, and feelings toward immigrants persist across immigrant waves, hence the conversation about representation cannot be ignored.

Janks (2012) in the epigraph espouses the importance of critical literacy in education whether we live in a peaceful society or one that is fraught by conflict or war. Elsewhere, Janks (2013) delineated that a critical approach to literacy comes with the understanding that "words are not innocent, but instead work to position us" (p. 227).

Thus, critical literacy empowers students to "*read* both the word and the world in relation to power, identity, difference and access to knowledge, skills, tools and resources" (p. 227). As students learn to be critical consumers of their world, it is important to share fiction and nonfiction stories with them, stories that go deeper than "this is so cute!"

The publication of stories of immigrant experiences has increased in the last decade, with a greater number of nonfiction stories for young children and adolescents highlighting tales of travels to the United States, Canada, and the United Kingdom. Many of these stories differ from earlier stories of immigration in that they offer the unvarnished truth about the immigrant experience, from voluntary immigrants, to refugees, to undocumented families who leave their homelands for various reasons in search of a better life for their families.

This chapter focuses on three such stories, nonfiction stories that present the other side of the immigrant experience. Ann Bausum's (2009) informational book, *Denied, Detained, Deported: Stories from the Dark Side of American Immigration*, explores stories of immigrants who were refused entry into or were deported from the United States. *Mohammed's Journey: A Refugee Diary* (2009), by Anthony Robinson, Annemarie Young, and June Allen, narrates the journey of young Mohammed and his mother from Iraq to gaining asylum in Great Britain. The third book, a graphic novel by G.B.

Tran (2011), *Vietnamerica: A Family's Journey*, relates Tran's family's survival during the Vietnam War and their eventual resettlement in the United States as refugees. Together, these three texts highlight the importance of discussing narratives that have largely been neglected or vilified across grade levels.

Students should not have to wait until reaching a specific grade to broaden their understandings of immigrant and refugee experiences. As these texts span the kindergarten to twelfth-grade spectrum, they provide teachers with scaffolded building blocks to ensure that all students have access to such texts.

In the remainder of this chapter, we argue for a critical stance to incorporating and dialoging about nonfiction literature in the literacy classroom, including these three examples, to help students understand issues of social justice and the impact on immigration across diverse immigrant groups.

We offer two vignettes of Kate and Cody's experiences of pairing nonfiction with fiction stories about immigrant issues in their language arts classes. Like Flowers and Flowers (2009), the coauthors of this chapter believe that incorporating nonfiction stories in the curricula can be meaningful in helping students connect to their lived experiences and others around them.

IMPORTANCE OF IMMIGRANT STORIES: UNFOLDING THE MULTICULTURAL UMBRELLA

According to Short, Lynch-Brown, and Tomlinson (2013), multicultural literature refers to literature, regardless of genre, about people within a particular culture. It is also more narrowly described as literature by and about groups that have been marginalized by the dominant European-American culture in the United States. Bishop (1997) posits that the definition of multicultural literature should be comprehensive and inclusive, incorporating "books that reflect the racial, ethnic, and social diversity that is characteristic of our pluralistic society and of the world" (p. 3).

Multicultural literature offers opportunities to promote the interaction of the readers across ethnic lines, helping readers to interact, reflect, think creatively and critically, increase their cultural awareness, decrease ethnocentrism, and create a global perspective (Cliff & Miller, 1997).

Immigrant literature, enfolded under the broader umbrella of multicultural literature, is "literature that depicts the experiences of various immigrant groups" (Lowery, 2003, p. 19). The Standards for the English Language Arts (National Council of Teachers of English & the International Reading Association, 1996) require the incorporation of diverse texts representing a variety of cultural experiences into the language arts curriculum. Immigrant literature, then, gives teachers the tools to learn about their diverse students and to help all students in their classrooms to learn about the real world outside their lived experiences.

Denied, Detained, Deported, an informational book, opens with two poems that address notions of liberty and freedom in the United States. The book goes on to explore multiple immigration stories of ordinary people's experiences; for example, Herb Karliner, a twelve-year-old boy who was denied asylum after fleeing Nazi Germany. Some Jewish refugees on the *St. Louis* attempted suicide off the coast of Cuba after they were denied asylum. Another story explores the experiences of Emma Goldman, called "Red Emma," who was forced to leave the United States because her view of labor laws was not consistent with what many considered "American values."

The mandates that led to the Japanese internment camps of World War II and the experiences of migrant workers and Chinese immigrants are highlighted. Photographs, timelines, and quotes punctuate multiple tales of immigration throughout US history. Readers get to explore the often-undiscussed history of immigration and policies in the United States in this powerful book.

Mohammed's Journey: A Refugee Diary explores the story of Mohammed, an Iraqi child born in the Kurdish region of the country. His story is brought to life through illustrations and accompanying photographs. Images and text are arranged in a scrapbook-like format that adds a layer of intimacy to the reading experience. The account is written in a very straightforward manner that allows readers to step into Mohammed's shoes and explore what it means to be a refugee.

Mohammed's story includes the loss of his father, who was beaten and removed from the family home by soldiers. Mohammed and his mother then endured a harrowing journey through dangerous terrain and multiple countries to reach Great Britain. Despite his experiences, Mohammed remains an optimistic child full of hope for the future. The diary is intended for British audiences; however, the refugee experiences in the text are easily paralleled with current resettlement stories in the United States and Canada.

Finally, in *Vietnamerica: A Family's Journey*, Tran writes and illustrates the emotional and honest story of his family's survival through war in Vietnam and their eventual resettlement in the United States as refugees. The images are incredibly detailed, and the use of color heightens the emotion and tension present throughout the text. Like many immigrant children, Tran is not fully aware of his family's journey to the United States and their previous life in Vietnam. Tran comes of age in the United States and always feels slightly different from his parents. He struggles to understand his parents, their relationship, and his family history. It is not until he reaches adulthood that he begins to make sense of his family's backstory.

Though each tale represents a different time period, the traumatic experiences are painful and seem to eclipse time and place. In *Denied, Detained,*

Deported, some immigrants arrive in the United States seeking refuge from the turmoil in their homelands. However, some are denied entry and others, who speak out against horrific treatments, are branded and deported. Many years later, Tran and his family seek refuge in the United States because of the war that ravaged their Vietnamese homeland.

And still later, war causes Mohammed and his mother to seek refuge in the United Kingdom. Hence, across time, place, and space, factors cause people to leave their homelands in search of a better life. For many, like Syrian refugees in recent years, the decision to leave their homes is predominantly caused by political and/or economic issues.

BEING CRITICAL ABOUT SOCIAL JUSTICE

While much has been written about social justice and education (Hytten & Bettez, 2011), there still needs to be a concerted effort by teacher educators and scholars to help teachers employ a critical lens in their curriculum to ensure students understand notions of equity and justice. Alsup and Miller (2014) argue that teacher educators, particularly literacy teachers, need to be well-versed in ideas related to social justice, because equity and the ability to understand others are key factors for teachers working with diverse students in today's schools. Banks (2006) states that a "thoughtful citizenry" is necessary for the "creation and survival of a democratic society" (p. 141).

Therefore, teaching with a social justice perspective can better prepare students for such a society. While many definitions of social justice education exist, Bell (2007) provides a comprehensive definition:

> We believe that social justice is both a process and a goal. The goal of social justice is full and equal participation of all groups in a society that is mutually shaped to meet their needs. Social justice includes a vision of society in which the distribution of resources is equitable and all members are physically and psychologically safe and secure. We envision a society in which individuals are both self-determining (able to develop their full capacities) and interdependent (capable of interacting democratically with others). Social justice involved social actors who have a sense of their own agency as well as a sense of social responsibility toward and with others, their society, and the broader world in which we live. These are conditions we wish not only for our own society but also for every society in our interdependent global community. (pp. 1–2)

The authors of this chapter believe that teaching for social justice is a constructive way to encourage students to be better informed and critical citizens who work toward a more equitable society.

One way that teachers can include a social justice perspective in their classrooms is by employing literature that reflects the very ideas that they wish their students to understand. Students develop a better understanding and appreciation of others by learning through a variety of texts (Bickmore, 2008). Baer and Glasgow (2010) state that, "Just as people are afraid of the dark, because it contains the unknown, people are often afraid of unknown peoples and cultures" (p. 24). Therefore, by exposing students to other cultures and worldviews through literature and nonfiction texts, teachers can nurture student understandings of other people and groups.

The impact literature can have on helping students to develop more critical lenses and social justice dispositions can be supplemented when paired with quality nonfiction texts. Beach, Thein, and Parks (2008) suggest the combination of "concrete materials" with multicultural literature can "function to help students recognize how aspects of everyday life are influenced by racist discourses and cultural models" (pp. 264–65).

"Concrete materials" can be imagined as nonfiction articles that highlight the lived experiences of humans. Additionally, Webb (2009) calls for incorporating nonfiction texts to supplement the teaching of literature from predominantly Muslim countries to support students' understanding of cultural values and norms that are different from their own, especially for students whose only exposure to the predominantly Muslim countries is through singular and stereotypical narratives perpetuated in news media.

One can abstract this argument out and apply it to exploring the cultural values and norms of any society, including students' own. Bean and Harper (2006) note that critical readings have the power to disrupt the "status quo." Finally, Appleman (2014) argues that students should learn to apply critical literary theory to both fictional and nonfictional texts in order to analyze how ideology is embedded within texts and the world around them. Table 3.1 offers simple suggestions that teachers can incorporate in their curriculum to extend the conversation after reading books about the immigrant experience with their students.

Teachers can also ask students to extend their understandings of notions of justice by using themes from their assigned fictional readings and exploring how these concepts relate to contemporary issues. For example, Glasgow (2001) suggests the use of *Declaration of Human Rights* as a text for students to understand that all people are entitled to certain rights.

Additionally, Simmons (2012) paired social justice issues like hunger and inequality present in the fictional text *The Hunger Games* (Collins, 2010) with actionable projects related to real-world contemporary issues to help students extend their learning from the fictional world to the "real" one. Such activities, again, allow teachers more opportunities to incorporate nonfictional texts into their classes.

The selection of which texts teachers will use is extremely important. Therefore, the selection of engaging texts is the first step. Teachers cannot expect the texts to automatically result in students' growing a social justice

Advocating for Immigrant Experiences in Nonfiction Literature

Table 3.1. Teaching Suggestions for Expanding Classroom Discussion

After reading the suggested texts, students can extend their knowledge through digital interactions. A reading of a text does not have to be limited to the text itself; instead, teachers can encourage and extend student learning by incorporating additional nonfiction texts, videos, and images.

- Students can research Teaching Tolerance's timelines of different immigrant groups.
- Students can explore the Library of Congress pages that detail additional information about immigration and specific groups.
- PBS Education has a variety of videos, images, and audio clips about immigration and refugee experiences that teachers and students can explore together.
- Students can review the backstory of *The Voyage of the St. Louis*, at the National Holocaust Museum website.
- Students can explore stories and texts associated with the Smithsonian Institute's traveling exhibit *The Bittersweet Harvest: The Bracero Project*. The project focuses on migrant farmworkers' stories.
- Students can explore the Smithsonian's interactive storytelling experience through its website that explores Japanese American internment camp experiences.

perspective. Indeed, teachers must also craft and implement curriculum that supports students' development of critical literacy.

Janks (2013) posits that critical literacy pedagogy must address power, diversity, access, and design/redesign through an integrated approach that sees the four elements as intertwined and reinforcing; otherwise, students will not have a full understanding of how complex sociopolitical issues are interdependent in our world. Janks concludes that a critical literacy pedagogy will always be important. Therefore, it is important for teachers to share their experiences using these frameworks to help others as they foster critical literacy and social justice perspectives for their students.

TEACHERS IN ACTION: SCAFFOLDING CLASSROOM EXPERIENCES

The two vignettes presented in this chapter share stories of Kate and Cody engaging students in their English language arts classrooms in critical discussions about immigration and social justice themes. As their students sought answers to their burgeoning questions about the state of immigration in the United States, both teachers set out to find materials that were available and that they each felt would not simply answer their students' questions but would stimulate critical discussions.

Textbox 3.1

Classroom Vignette 1: Kate

My second year of teaching, I was asked to teach strictly from the outdated textbooks stacked in dusty piles in the back of my classroom. I came to school early one morning and sat in the dark, windowless storage space and searched for a class set of nonfiction texts that I could use instead of the assigned textbook. Luckily, I located a stack of newer copies of Elie Wiesel's autobiographical account of *Night* (2006). Elie Wiesel eventually became an American citizen. Therefore, every year I taught the book to my students and we considered the different stories of American immigrants and refugees. I shared my grandfather's immigration story, and some students shared what they knew about their own family's history in the United States.

One afternoon, I walked between the rows of desks reading the words aloud that detailed Elie's treacherous train ride to Auschwitz after he was deported from his home. Although I read softly, my voice echoed throughout the room because my students listened with such intensity. Students engaged in a visualization and were only permitted to use pen, crayon, or pencil for the activity. One student shaded his entire paper using long straight lines and smudged the thick layers of graphite to look like smoke rising into the night sky. Another student complained that she was not artistic, but she drew darkened boxes to represent trains and fire consuming them. After school, some students and I taped each and every drawing from three different class periods to the back wall. I can remember my first students of the morning walking into the classroom the next day. The room only had a few box windows along one wall and a little light peeped through the windows. Because the room was sticky with humidity, the papers had wilted slightly overnight. But the students stood in amazement at the different drawings they'd created based on the text.

Over the years, the lessons evolved beyond teaching the background history of *Night* and what happened to Elie Wiesel and grew to include historical facts and stories I didn't think my students were familiar with. Soon after I started teaching *Night*, I was hired at a different school. I wanted the history surrounding the text to be more tangible. So, before we began the memoir, I would reserve the library so that each student could access a computer. Using our class website, I outlined an interactive digital tour of the National Holocaust Museum. Students picked any three exhibits from the educational portion of the website. I cautioned students to only select what they were emotionally comfortable exploring. Our library allowed students to reserve sound-canceling headphones, and so many students wore the large black devices over their heads. I would walk up and down the rows of glowing screens, the room again silent with students engaged in their digital explorations. Sometimes a student would reach up and grab my arm, or wave a hand for me to come over to them. I would kneel on the rough carpet and whisper to the students. "What did you look at? Oh, really? Why did you pick that exhibit? What did you learn?"

Another year, I projected a black-and-white picture of a Japanese internment camp on the board; students were asked to free-write what they believed was happening in the picture. After a few moments, I opened the floor to class discussion, and Elizabeth (pseudonym), always an eager participant in my first period, raised her hand. "Yes, Elizabeth, what did you write?" She shared a vivid description of a concentration camp. "See there, the endless stacks of barracks where they kept the Jewish prisoners." Similar impressions were shared by peers. When I revealed that the image was from the Midwestern United States, the tension in the room grew palpable. Elizabeth stood up and banged her hand on the desk. "Wait, are you saying we locked people up?" After I shared some more background information and we watched a short historic clip from the History Channel, Elizabeth raised her hand again. "Why is this the first time we are learning about this? We're in tenth grade." She was practically hissing with disbelief. Some peers were shaking their heads and muttering in support. I asked her, "Great question. Why is that, do you think?" The class completely devolved into angry chaos as students shouted their answers.

Textbox 3.2
Classroom Vignette 2: Cody

During the summer after my first year teaching at a developmental research school, I realized that, despite my best effort, my curriculum suffered from a lack of immigrant voices. I wanted to amend that error by incorporating multiple types of texts into the curriculum that spoke to the experiences of immigrants and the children of immigrants within our nation while avoiding painting immigration experiences as monolithic. I used multiple texts of different mediums and authors, including a then newly minted television show on ABC.

Fresh Off the Boat, a television show adapted from celebrity chef Eddie Huang's memoir of the same name that documents his life as a child of Taiwanese immigrants, proved to be a powerful text for helping students better explore the experiences of immigrants. We read the graphic novel *American Born Chinese*, which follows the fictional story of a Chinese American student named Jin, alongside *Fresh Off the*

Boat while tracing the ways Anglophonic, white, middle-class culture is embedded, often invisibly, within school systems and our broader culture. Both Jin and Eddie are the children of immigrants. We traced our understandings of culture by noting language uses in school in both the graphic novel and television show. Then we documented how the white students reacted to the characters' food, family traditions, and communication styles in ways that often left Eddie and Jin marginalized.

This activity took several class periods and included multiple episodes of the television show, including the pilot episode, which highlights how Eddie's family moved from Washington, District of Columbia, to Orlando, Florida. Additionally, we watched the episode "Success Perm," which addresses how beauty standards in the United States are often wrapped around images frequently associated with white Americans, which was a theme echoed in *American Born Chinese*. Finally, we watched the episode "Philip Goldstein," in which the titular Chinese American guest character frequently disrupts assumptions made about him based on his race due to the fact that he is adopted by conservative Jewish parents. The assumption that individuals of the same race will automatically be friends is found in both the television show and the graphic novel. Students began to make connections between the two texts that reveal their own assumptions being questioned.

At the end of the lesson, students wrote across the two texts to explore how being caught between the dominant culture of schooling and family cultures affected the two characters, Eddie and Jin. The activity required students to broaden their understanding of "text." *Fresh Off the Boat* is a television show that is nonfiction as it draws its inspiration from the memoir of the same title, whereas *American Born Chinese* is a fictional graphic novel. Neither "texts" were traditional books. Students took note of this. "I like how the television show helps me understand culture clashes between them," Gavin informed me, and Vanessa wrote that the combination of the fictional graphic novel with the nonfiction television show helped her "understand complex issues that we need to be talking about in schools."

READING FOR SELF AND CHANGE: EXPLORING IMMIGRANT EXPERIENCES

Children's literature helps students become better readers, make connections with text and their own lives, and learn about historical figures and different cultures. However, it can serve another important purpose: It can be a way to show students how children like them all over the world work toward helping others and being agents of change, exemplifying social justice.

The two teacher vignettes provide a sampling of this practice as we see students learning about diverse experiences, yet they become critical consumers, seeking to understand why things happen the way they do and offering suggestions for how they can be different.

Likewise, the three immigrant stories highlighted provide great models for encouraging students to query how difference is actualized across immigrant periods, how children like them are often caught in the crossfires of war and dissent, and what they can do to make a difference in their space and time. Short (2011) determines that children's books can be reflective for children and that they can make connections to life experiences in and outside themselves on global and local levels. Moreover, books can help them understand how they would like to be treated, and thus they can take action to make a difference in their lives and for others.

Al-Hazza (2010) argues for ensuring that teachers do not forget a key component that students bring to their learning, their reading experience. "The meaning of the printed word is not just what is written on the page but is also created from the meaning that the reader brings to the text" (p. 63). Morrell and Morrell (2012) also posit that students should see diverse examples of themselves in the books they read, determining that "when we think about multicultural readings of texts we should encourage students not only to tap into their own cultural reservoirs, but they should also practice reading texts from the perspectives of others" (p. 12).

Students learn to make sense of the world around them as they learn about others who may have parallel experiences. Kate and Cody's teaching practices of engaging students with unfamiliar experiences give testament to this truth.

CONCLUSION

Issues of social justice become more urgent as the representation of varying immigrant groups and others become more negatively maligned in the media and elsewhere. It is a global issue, which is more frequently reflected in nonfiction children's and young adult literature. O'Neil (2010) determines that, "at the heart of social justice is the realization that things do not have to continue as they are but can be changed, and that this change occurs only when individuals act to create it" (p. 48).

Discussion about social justice, how we see it and how it is determined, becomes more important as teachers attempt to answer their students' questions about the images that bombard them. Students are more likely to be in global classrooms with peers who come from different ethnic, cultural, and socioeconomic backgrounds. They often compare themselves with each other and find their worth in what they have and how they are treated. Thus, it is important for teachers to help them effectively negotiate the spaces they inhabit.

It is vital for teachers to incorporate nonfiction texts that portray diverse experiences for their students. These stories can embolden students to take action, as they realize that they, too, have the power to make a change in the world. Reading nonfiction literature about others' experience, whether local, national, or international, can provide efferent or aesthetic experiences. It is also important to allow students to dialogue about their reading experiences and to share their views. Finally, nonfiction literature has the power to make a difference, one story at a time.

REFERENCES

Al-Hazza, T. (2010). Motivating disengaged readers through multicultural children's literature. *New England Reading Association Journal, 45*(2), 63–68.

Alsup, J., and Miller, S. J. (2014). Reclaiming English education: Rooting social justice in dispositions. *English Education, 46*(3), 195–215.

Appleman, D. (2014). *Critical encounters in secondary English: Teaching literary theory to adolescents* (3rd ed.). New York, NY: Teachers College Press.

Banks, J. A. (2006). Democracy, diversity, and social justice: Educating citizens for the public interest in a global age. In G. Ladson-Billings and W. F. Tate (eds.), *Education research in the public interest: Social justice, action, and policy* (pp. 141–57). New York, NY: Teachers College Press.

Baer, A.L., and Glasgow, J. N. (2010). Negotiating understanding through the young adult literature of Muslim cultures. *Journal of Adolescent & Adult Literacy, 54*(1), 23–32.

Beach, R., Thein, A. H., and Parks, D. (2008). *High school students' competing social worlds: Negotiating identities and allegiances in response to multicultural literature*. New York, NY: Lawrence Erlbaum Associates.

Bean, T. W., and Harper, H. J. (2006). Exploring notions of freedom in and through young adult literature. *Journal of Adolescent & Adult Literacy, 50*(2), 96–104.

Bell, L. A. (2007). Theoretical foundations for social justice education. In M. Adams, L.A. Bell, and P. Griffin (eds). *Teaching for diversity and social justice* (2nd ed.), (pp. 1–14). New York, NY: Routledge.

Bickmore, S. T. (2007). It is inexcusable to deny inexcusable a place in the classroom. *The ALAN Review, 35*(2), 75–83.

Bishop, R. S. (1997). Selecting literature for a multicultural curriculum. In V. J. Harris (ed.), *Using multiethnic literature in the k-8 classroom* (pp. 1–19). Norwood, MA: Christopher-Gordon.

Cliff, C., and Miller, S. (1997). *Multicultural dialogue in literature-history classes: The dance of creative and critical thinking (7.9)*. Albany, NY: National Research Center on English Learning and Achievement.

Costello, M. (2016). *The Trump effect: The impact of the presidential election on our nation's schools*. Rep. Montgomery: Southern Poverty Law Center. Print.

Flowers, T., and Flowers, L. (2009). Nonfiction in the early grades: Making reading and writing relevant for all students. *Journal for the Liberal Arts and Sciences, 13*(2), 40–50.

Glasgow, J. N. (2001). Teaching social justice through young adult literature. *English Journal, 90*(6), 54–61.

Hytten, K., and Bettez, S.C. (2011). Understanding education for social justice. *Educational Foundations, 25*(1/2), 7–24.

Janks, H. (2012). The importance of critical literacy. *English Teaching: Practice and Critique*, *11*(1), 150–63.
Janks, H. (2013). Critical literacy in teaching and research. *Education Inquiry*, *4*(2), 225–42.
Lowery, R. M. (2000). *Immigrants in children's literature*. New York, NY: Peter Lang.
Lowery, R. M. (2003). Reading *The Star Fisher*: Toward critical and sociological interpretations of immigrant literature. *Multicultural Education*, *10*(3), 19–23.
Morrell, E., and Morrell, J. (2012). Multicultural readings of multicultural literature and the promotion of social awareness in ELA classrooms. *New England Reading Association Journal*, *47*(2), 10–16.
National Council of Teachers of English and International Reading Association. (1996). *Standards for the English language arts*. Newark, DE: International Reading Association.
O'Neil, K. (2010). Once upon today: Teaching for social justice with postmodern picturebooks. *Children's Literature in Education*, *41*(1), 40–51.
Short, K. G. (2011). Children taking action within global inquiries. *The Dragon Lode*, *29*(2), 50–59.
Short, K. G., Lynch-Brown, C. M., and Tomlinson, C. M. (2013). *Essentials of children's literature* (8th ed.). New York, NY: Pearson.
Simmons, A. M. (2012). Class on fire: Using the *Hunger Games* trilogy to encourage social action. *Journal of Adolescent & Adult Literacy*, *56*(1), 22–34.
Webb, A. (2009). Literature from the modern Middle East: Making a living connection. *English Journal*, *98*(3), 80–89.

CHILDREN'S AND YOUNG ADULT BOOKS CITED

Bausum, A. (2009). *Denied, detained, deported: Stories from the dark side of American immigration*. Washington, DC: National Geographic.
Collins, S. (2010). *The hunger games*. New York, NY: Scholastic.
Robinson, A., Young, A., and Allan, J. (2009). *Mohammed's journey: A refugee diary*. United Kingdom: Frances Lincoln.
Tran, G. B. (2011). *Vietnamerica: A family's journey*. New York, NY: Villard.
Wiesel, E. (2006). *Night*. New York, NY: Hill and Wang.
Yang, G. L. (2006). *American Born Chinese*. New York, NY: Square Fish.

Chapter Four

Teaching for Social Justice

Nonfiction Texts and Multigenre Writing

Ann Berger-Knorr and Mary Napoli

Dear Reader,

    A wise college professor once told me, "Good literature asks us to think, wonder, reflect, and imagine." This multigenre writing project has given me the opportunity to fully understand exactly what it means to write and feel literature from an author's perspective. Although I have always appreciated excellent literature, I never understood how empowering it was to create your own work through thinking, wondering, reflecting, and imagination. This project is a collection of works relating to Ruby Bridges and her path to school every day.

    The repetend I have chosen for this particular project is "Ruby Bridges is one of the bravest children in history." . . . It is important to try to understand the perspective of Ruby Bridges and the struggles she dealt with [which] no six-year-old should ever undergo. The purpose of this project was to explore the ideas and thoughts of onlookers and supporters of her cause. Ruby was on the forefront of integration and desegregation of schools, which is a lot to ask of such a young child. . . . As you read through this project, I want you to keep in mind the bravery of this young, six-year-old child and how she impacted both the adults and children around her.

–Anna's Introduction to the multigenre writing project (pseudonyms used throughout)

BACKGROUND

Like us, many teacher educators take seriously their commitment of teaching for diversity and social justice. Through their teaching, writing, mentoring, and other scholarly pursuits, they work tirelessly and passionately to find ways to model and espouse democratic values with their students, preservice teachers. As teacher educators, we have explored with course projects grounded in diverse literature, critical literacy, and social justice so as to model for our students the possibilities of a truly literate, empowered, and civic-minded citizenry and society. One such project that exemplifies a conceptualization of teaching for social justice is the multigenre writing project.

For the past several years in our literacy and literature methods course, preservice teachers have been required to complete a multigenre writing project contextualized within a literature-based/writing workshop framework of literacy instruction. The idea behind the project is to utilize literature as a springboard for discussing important social issues and encourage students to write about those issues as a form of literature response.

Utilizing grand conversations and literature circles as a starting point for the project, students are asked to discuss important topics related to the world—around a social justice theme—and explore those topics through a variety of writing genres, including narrative, descriptive, poetry, expository, biographical, and persuasive genres of writing.

Along the way, students are provided opportunities to read and write critically as well as consider ways social justice can be incorporated into an elementary curriculum. In the end, the multigenre writing project affords students critical opportunities to "find their voices" and showcase themselves as empowered readers and writers both in and out of school.

Various genres have been used in the past to drive the multigenre writing project, tapping both contemporary realistic fiction and historical fiction novels. However, this past semester students were required to read high-quality nonfiction texts as a basis for the project. Nonfiction books for this project were selected from those that have been included on the Jane Addams Children's Book Award (JACBA) lists.

As Griffith (2013) notes, the JACBA award acknowledges books "about struggles for social justice past and present, stories about people who devote their lives to fighting injustice, and stories about the importance of working together collectively and nonviolently" (p. 49).

Thus, in the project, students were provided choice among a variety of award-winning JACBA nonfiction texts and topics including worker's rights, human rights, civil rights, desegregation, equal rights, and voting rights. Consequently, themes of social justice underscored all the texts chosen for the project. The above "Dear Reader" letter highlights the introduction to one student's multigenre writing project utilizing the nonfiction text *Through My Eyes* by Ruby Bridges (1999).

This chapter captures an exemplary example of a multigenre social justice writing project, as it showcases the capacity in future teachers to consider multiple perspectives, challenge dominant narratives, and develop a heightened awareness of themselves, others, and society as a whole. The project creates an important space and opportunity for preservice teachers to discuss issues of social injustice and to respond critically both through reading and writing, in multiple ways.

WHAT IS SOCIAL JUSTICE?

According to Bell (2007), social justice can be defined as both a process and a goal. "The goal of social justice is full and equal participation of all groups in a society that is mutually shaped to meet their needs" (p. 1). It includes "a vision of society in which the distribution of resources is equitable and all members are physically and psychologically safe and secure" (p. 2). The process for attaining the goal of social justice should be fair and equitable involving individuals who have a sense of their own agency as well as a sense of responsibility towards others and broader society.

In a similar vein, social justice education can be conceptualized as both a theoretical construct as well as a pedagogical practice. Within collaborative and democratic classrooms, both teachers and students critically examine the world in search of opportunities for social action and social change. Thus, at its very core, a social justice education interrogates systems of power and privilege and seeks to answer why things are the way they are and what courses of actions might be taken to make the world a better place.

There are numerous pedagogical frameworks for social justice education available in the literature (see, for example, Adams, 2007; Hackman, 2008; Bigelow, 2004; and Wade, 2004).

Picower (2012) offers a framework for implementing social justice in the classroom that can be easily adapted to kindergarten to twelfth-grade settings. Incorporating six elements of social justice into a curriculum design, the framework provides a more practical and teacher-friendly approach to social justice teaching. Below, we highlight Picower's (2012) six elements of social justice:

1. Self-Love and Knowledge
2. Respect for Others
3. Issues of Social Injustice
4. Social Movements and Social Change
5. Awareness Raising
6. Social Action

By incorporating the elements of social justice into the classroom, students develop a better understanding of themselves, a deeper appreciation of others, and a greater consideration for ways in which to take action in their lives. While it is not necessary to incorporate all the elements in the classroom at one time, they should be addressed throughout the year, as students develop tools for social action (Picower, 2012).

CREATING SPACES FOR CRITICAL CONVERSATIONS ON ISSUES OF SOCIAL JUSTICE USING NONFICTION TEXTS

Nonfiction texts that offer accounts or histories of social movements and/or social change are particularly fitting for discussing issues of social justice. Embedded in these texts are "multiple histories, narratives, perspectives, and truths" that are ripe for "unpack[ing] critical issues within historical contexts" (Polleck, 2016, p. 61). Such texts not only deepen students' understanding of history, they provide important opportunities for students to experience, vicariously, everyday people fighting against injustice.

Along the way, students are granted opportunities to connect with diverse "others," examine relations of power, and consider how they, too, as individuals might work for social change. Books such as these can provide "powerful demonstrations" (Short, Giorgis, & Lowery, 2013, p. 32) of people taking action and making a difference in the world.

In one sense, social justice nonfiction texts can be viewed as "instruments of power" (Ching, 2005, p. 135). As "critical texts" (Riley & Crawford-Garret, 2016), they not only deepen students' understanding of history, themselves, and "others"; they situate the examination of power and injustice within a broader conversation of what it means to live and participate in a democratic society as engaged and informed citizens.

THE PROJECT

In the spring semester of 2017, forty-nine predominantly white, middle-class preservice teachers enrolled in a literacy methods course were invited to develop multigenre writing projects around a social justice theme. To begin, nonfiction book talks were presented about the following Jane Addams Children's Book Award selections: *Brave Girl* by Michelle Markel (2013); *Separate Is Never Equal* by Duncan Tonatiuh (2014); *Through My Eyes* by Ruby Bridges (1999); *Martin's Big Words* by Doreen Rappaport (2001); and *Claudette Colvin: Twice Toward Justice* by Phillip Hoose (2009).

Students were then asked to form literature discussion groups based on their chosen text utilizing literature circle roles. Literature circles, as noted by Harvey Daniels (2002), are not limited to just fiction texts, but can be adapted for well-written expository texts (p. 8) to enhance both literacy and content connections (see Daniels, 2006, p. 13). While the preservice teachers were familiar with traditional literature circle roles, the roles were adapted in the following ways so that issues of social justice were at the heart of their conversations.

Textbox 4.1
Literature Circle Roles and Responsibilities
with Nonfiction Texts

Literature Circle Roles (adapted for nonfiction)	Student Responsibility
Discussion Leader	Prepares a list of questions to support further investigations and inquiry about specific social issue(s) related to the text.
Social Issues Connector	Provides insights into how the text relates to his/her life through historical and contemporary contexts. The Social Issues Connector also identifies interdisciplinary connections, suggests further inquiries, and locates supporting sources (i.e., news, blogs, videos, local events, historical and contemporary examples) about the social issue to share with group members.
The Passage Master	Marks sentences, phrases, or quotes from the text that catch their attention during reading and that they believe to be worthy of future discussion. Such passages should help students further their understanding of a particular social issue, movement, person, or time period.
Text Set Locator	Identifies additional texts (both digital, print, or community resources) that enhance the overarching social issue or theme. The Text Set Locator discusses how the texts connect to the focal nonfiction selection and social issue(s).
Word Wizard	Identifies content-specific words and vocabulary that are critical to the meaning of the text and help readers better understand a particular concept, issue, person, or time period.
Multimodal Archivist	Locates digital resources (e.g., podcasts, videos, songs, etc.) about the social justice theme, issue, person, or time period. The Archivist works with the other group members to develop a group Padlet to archive various resources to facilitate further discussion and to serve as inspiration for their multigenre writing project.

In addition to utilizing literature circle roles, students were also presented with several critical response invitations during class sessions to expand their thinking and consideration of texts in a myriad of ways. For example, in one class invitation, students were familiarized with the tenets of critical literacy and presented with a series of questions as a way to help them examine underlying assumptions and power relations within texts.

In order to help students take an active role in the reading process and to raise awareness regarding the political nature of texts, critical question-posing was modeled for the class (Leland, Lewison, & Harste, 2013; Lewison, Flint & Van Zluys, 2002). Similar to that of Jones (2006), students were encouraged to "peel away the layers [of texts] through consideration of perspective, power and positioning" (as cited by Riley & Crawford, p. 95).

In doing so, students were challenged to examine the perspective from which stories were told, whose interests were served as a result, and the role social and cultural forces played in shaping the stories, lives, and experiences of the characters involved in the texts.

In another class invitation coined "Windows, Mirrors, and Sliding Glass Doors" (inspired by Rudine Sims Bishop's [1990] seminal article by the same name), students were encouraged to read their texts first as a *window* "offering views of the world that may be real or imagined" and as a *sliding glass door* to "walk through, in imagination, to become part of whatever world has been created or recreated by the author." Next, students were asked to consider their text as *mirror* and reflect on their own life experiences "as part of the larger human experience."

Through this inquiry-based invitation, students were provided opportunities to see the world and experiences from the perspective of "others" and (re)think the importance of "other" in their own identity constructions. Moving back and forth between multiple positions of, for example, "Who are you and what experiences have you had in the world?" and "Who am I and what experiences have I had?" is a consciousness-raising process that often prompts students to (re)consider who they are in relation to diverse others and the role power plays in forming human relations.

In the next phase of the project, students were introduced to multigenre writing via an Annenberg video featuring Dr. Tom Romano (http://www.learner.org/workshops/middlewriting/p5_tr_audio.html). Multigenre writing invites students to conduct research and write across a range of genres (Allen, 2001; Allen & Swistak, 2004; Mack, 2002, 2015; Romano, 2000) while considering multiple perspectives about a topic. Multigenre projects arise from research, experience, and imagination (Romano, 2000, pp. x–xi), and contain texts in which "each piece of the paper [project] utilizes a different genre, reveals one facet of the topic, and makes its own point" (Allen, 2001, p. 2).

Throughout the multigenre writing project, preservice teachers were encouraged to weave recurring themes, images, symbols, phrases, or quotes, known as repetends, throughout their pieces. The purpose of repetend is to create unity among the various genre pieces.

In addition to watching the Annenberg video, preservice teachers read about multigenre writing in their writing methods course textbook and peer-reviewed journal articles. Using *Teaching Writing: Balancing Process and Product* (Tompkins, 2012), prospective teachers peer-taught chapters on various writing genres and shared with each other pertinent information regarding the teaching of writing genres with elementary- and middle-school-aged students.

On specific days, our students were provided in-class time to write and work on drafts of various pieces related to a specific genre for inclusion in their multigenre projects. In all, the preservice teachers were asked to write a total of eight pieces (including a multimedia piece) across six genres of writing: expository, narrative, descriptive, poetry, biographical, and persuasive.

While students were given considerable choice with respect to the form of these pieces, three specific pieces of writing were required. These included:

(1) An expository essay that grounded the social justice inquiry for the project;
(2) A persuasive letter (to raise awareness and prompt action); and
(3) A multimedia piece using a digital tool (e.g., Animoto, Piktochart, Little Bird Tales, etc.).

Students were asked to compile their projects in a creative fashion, organized with a table of contents, a Dear Reader letter (explaining each of their pieces in the project), and a one-page Final Reflection (describing what they had learned about themselves as a result of the overall project).

Students chose to display their multigenre projects in both digital and print forms. Some presented their projects in a three-dimensional mode, including posters, newspapers, or containers, such as a time capsule or lunch box. Below, we share pictures of some examples.

DISCOVERIES

Picower's (2012) framework and elements of social justice provided a lens through which to examine how our students addressed and incorporated issues of social justice in their projects. The analysis of the students' pieces, including their "Dear Reader" letter, and Final Reflections, indicated students' growing awareness of diverse and multiple perspectives as they navigated the writing process.

Asking students to engage in multigenre writing based on a social justice theme or repetend provided them with opportunities to tap elements of social

Figure 4.1. Student Examples of Multi-genre Projects. Students in the study.

justice in their projects on at least two different levels. First, it afforded students the opportunity to showcase elements of social justice through the various writing pieces that they wrote. Often, these products were driven and/ or influenced by the very nature of the writing genre itself. For example, expository writing allowed the students opportunities to share their awareness and understanding of a particular social movement and/or social issue and/or particular individuals involved with those movements or issues.

Narratives and descriptive pieces of writing written in the forms of diaries, letters, journals, and blogs, etc., often helped students to capture feelings of empathy, compassion, and/or respect for others. Various forms of poetry including I AM poems and I WISH poems or free verse poetry evoked similar types of writing and responses, allowing students opportunities to "walk in the shoes of others" and take on roles and perspectives of people different from themselves.

Biographies and memoirs often showcased students' understanding of an individual's identity, history, culture, experiences, and self-worth, whereas persuasive letters and essays often captured ways in which individuals took action in the world by voicing opinions and taking a stand for issues important in their lives.

Second, in order to produce the various multigenre pieces, the project, by its very nature, prompted students to work through the various elements of social justice through critical conversations while exploring a critical stance. Much like consciousness-raising, the discussions surrounding the nonfiction

Teaching for Social Justice 47

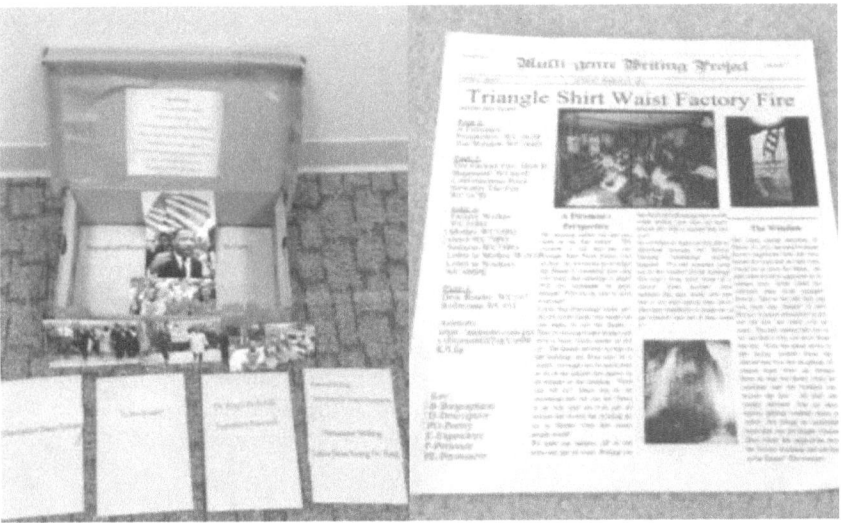

Figure 4.2. Student Examples of Multi-genre Projects. Students in the study.

texts helped the preservice teachers to deconstruct many of their taken-for-granted assumptions regarding history, power, people, and society, paving new ways of seeing and understanding.

By fostering a sense of awareness and agency, the multigenre writing project afforded students opportunities to rethink issues of social justice and (re)consider how they might live and act in the world. This was demonstrated in many of the "Dear Reader" letters and Fina; Reflection pieces written by our preservice teachers.

Although many of the pieces featured elements of social justice woven throughout their projects, below is an example of one student who captured each of Picower's (2012) elements of social justice across the entirety of her project. In this project, Anna (pseudonym) chose to read and respond to *Through My Eyes* by Ruby Bridges (1999). In this autobiographical account, readers follow Ruby's story—through her eyes—as one of the first African American children to be integrated into an all-white New Orleans public elementary school in 1960.

Through the project, Anna was inspired by the song "Ruby's Shoes" by Lori McKenna (2000) (https://www.youtube.com/watch?V=S-mCOTEsYHo) and the Norman Rockwell painting *The Problem We All Live With* (1964) (http://www.nrm.org/thinglink/text/ProblemLiveWith.html).

She developed her multigenre writing project in an attempt to "explore the ideas and thoughts of onlookers and supporters of [Ruby's] cause" and to show how Ruby "impacted both the adults and children around her" (as cited by Anna in her Dear Reader letter). Below is an interpretation of Anna's multigenre project and how she captured each of the six elements of social justice across her project.

Textbox 4.2
Anna's Incorporation of Six Elements of Social Justice in her Multigenre Writing

Self-Love and Knowledge

"Ruby"—Free Verse Poetry

Written from the perspective of Ruby, Anna's poem highlights Ruby's awareness of who she is in the world and of her treatment by others. Despite the realization that some people treat Ruby unfairly, Anna's poem evokes a powerful sense of self and self-worth as a human being, indicating a strong, positive identity on the part of Ruby.

Respect for Others

"The Diary of a New Orleans Teacher"—Personal Writing

Written from the perspective of Mrs. Henry (Ruby's white, first-grade teacher), Anna's diary entry depicts Mrs. Henry's love and respect for Ruby, despite the feelings and treatment of Ruby by others. Mrs. Henry's kind words and compassionate actions toward Ruby reveal her deeply held respect for Ruby.

Issues of Social Injustice

"From the Perspective of Norman Rockwell: An Observer"—Poetry

Written from the perspective of Norman Rockwell, Anna's poem captures the tension in Ruby's world between good and evil, light and darkness, equality and inequality, and violence and nonviolence as Ruby is escorted daily into the classroom by federal marshals.

Social Movements and Social Change

"NEW PRINT BY NORMAN ROCKWELL: *The Problem We All Live With*"

Written as an advertisement for Norman Rockwell's painting of the same name (http://www.nrm.org/thinglink/text/ProblemLiveWith.html), Anna's advertisement is a written attempt to convince people to buy Rockwell's painting depicting Ruby Bridges on her walk of integration. The painting portrays Ruby surrounded by federal marshals, in motion and moving forward, indicative of a larger social movement and societal change happening around her.

Raising Awareness

"Scene of Norman Rockwell and a Newspaper Editor"—Descriptive Writing

Written as a scene from a play, Anna juxtaposes two voices capturing the tension between two men: a newspaper editor and Norman Rockwell himself. Rockwell is fighting for change and is a strong proponent of desegregation.

> Deeply touched by Ruby's courage and actions, he wants to raise awareness in the people around him, shine a light upon hate, and wake the people up to the injustices happening around them.
>
> **Social Action**
>
> "A Letter from an Angry Educator"—Persuasive Writing
>
> In a persuasive letter, Anna takes on the role of Mrs. Henry, as Mrs. Henry takes deliberate action to initiate change in society by standing up for integration. As an educator, Mrs. Henry takes a stand and voices her opinion, as she advocates for the right of every child to receive an education, regardless of the color of their skin.

CONCLUSION

For teachers who wish to incorporate social justice nonfiction texts within their curriculum, they can carve spaces for "reading resistantly, communicating new lines of thinking, and pushing others to question how they come to see the world" (Van Sluys, 2005, pp. 22–23). Essentially, when kindergarten through twelfth-grade teachers invite their students to read texts from a critical perspective, they invite them to problematize their underlying assumptions, consider multiple perspectives, and become interrogators and analysts of texts. This active reading process not only supports the tenets of critical literacy, but also the overarching goals of English Language Arts Common Core State Standards (Dover, 2016).

As teachers navigate their literacy curriculum and support their students' curiosities about the real world, they will want to locate exemplary nonfiction selections to support such projects and may turn to award lists such as the Jane Addams Children's Book Award, National Council of Teachers of English Orbis Pictus Award for Outstanding Nonfiction for Children, and the Notable Social Studies Trade Books for Young People, to name a few.

Inviting students to question, comment, read, and write about social issues as part of the literacy curriculum can transform students' learning and understanding of themselves and broader society. Nonfiction social justice literature is one avenue to spark dialogue with students. Infusing nonfiction texts with social justice themes support interdisciplinary, student-driven, and inquiry-based instructional approaches and invite students to critically examine past and present histories, analyze multiple perspectives, and imagine possibilities of social change in the world.

Kindergarten through twelfth-grade teachers can incorporate similar multigenre writing projects based within a unit of study focused on social issues (e.g., environmentalism, poverty, equity, etc.). Multigenre writing provides students with the opportunity to navigate relevant topics, develop new understandings, formulate new questions, and compose personal responses across genres. This writing project has the capacity to instill a sense of student choice and ownership throughout the writing process to support student inquiries.

Although some educators may hesitate to infuse social justice teaching into their classrooms, or may be uncertain how best to tackle controversial or risky conversations about social issues, literature can help guide educators to engage their students in respectful and engaging dialogue.

As Short, Giorgis, and Lowery (2013) remark:

> Our challenge as educators . . . is to build on [students'] lived experiences through literature. Literature can invite [students] to explore multiple perspectives on social issues and develop the willingness and strategies for taking action. The complexity of these difficult issues must be addressed to move beyond talk about global issues into authentic and meaningful action for social change. Children and adolescents need perspective, not protection, as they consider who they are in the process of becoming and how they can make a difference. (p. 35)

Just as stories matter, so, too, does teaching for social justice matter. Using nonfiction literature with social justice themes and incorporating multigenre writing projects in the classroom provide powerful and transformative literacy engagements and have the potential to transform students' understandings of both self and world.

REFERENCES

Adams, M., Bell, L., and Griffin, P. (2007). *Teaching for diversity and social justice*. (second edition). New York, NY: Routledge: Taylor and Francis Group.

Allen, C. (2001). *The multigenre research paper: Voice, passion, and discovery in grades 4–6.* Portsmouth, NH: Heinemann.

Allen, C., and Swistak, L. (2004). Multigenre research: The power of choice and interpretation. *Language Arts, 81*(3), 223–32.

Bell, L. (2007). Theoretical foundations for social justice education. In M. Adams, L. Bell, and P. Griffin (Eds.), *Teaching for diversity and social justice: A sourcebook* (pp. 3–15). New York, NY: Routledge.

Bigelow, B., Harvey, B., Karp, S., and Miller, L. (2004) Introduction: Teaching for equity and justice. In B. Bigelow, B. Harvey, S. Karp, and L. Miller (Eds.), *Rethinking our classrooms. Teaching for equity and social justice* (Volume 2, pp. x–xl). Milwaukee, WI: Rethinking Schools.

Bishop, R.S. (1990). Mirrors, windows, and sliding glass doors. *Perspectives: Choosing and using books for the classroom, 6*(3), ix–x.

Ching, S. (2005). Multicultural children's literature as an instrument of power. *Language Arts, 83*(2), 128–36.

Common Core State Standards Initiative. (2010). Common Core State Standards for English language arts & literacy in history/social studies, science, and technical subjects. Washington, DC: National Governors Association.

Daniels, H. (2002). Expository text in literature circles. *Voices in the Middle, 9*(4), 7–14.

Daniels, H. (2006). What's the next big thing with literature circles? *Voices in the Middle, 13*(4), 10–15.

Griffith, S. (2013). *The Jane Addams Children's Book Award: Honoring children's literature for peace and social justice since 1953*. Lanham, MD: Scarecrow.

Hackman, H. (2005). Five essential components for social justice education. *Equity and Excellence in Education, 38*(2), 103–08.

Jones, S. (2006). *Girls, social class and literacy: What teachers can do to make a difference*. Portsmouth, NH: Heinemann.

Leland, C., Lewison, M., and Harste, J. (2013). *Teaching children's literature: It's critical!* New York, NY: Routledge.

Lewison M., Flint A.S., and Van Sluys K. (2002). Taking on critical literacy: The journey of newcomers and novices. *Language Arts, 79*(5), 382–92.

Mack, N. (2002). The ins, outs, and in-betweens of multigenre writing. *English Journal, 92*(2), 91–98.

Mack, N. (2015). *Engaging writers with multigenre research projects: A teacher's guide*. New York, NY: Teachers College Press.

Picower, B. (2012). Using their words: Six elements of social justice design for the elementary classroom. *International Journal of Multicultural Education, 14*(1), 1–17.

Polleck, J. (2016). Using nonfiction to advocate for change. *English Journal, 105*(4), 55–62.

Riley, K., and Crawford-Garrett, K. (2016). Critical texts in literacy teacher education: Living inquiries into racial justice and immigration. *Language Arts, 94*(2), 94–107.

Romano, T. (2000). *Blending genre, altering style: Writing multigenre papers*. Portsmouth, NH: Heinemann.

Short, K., Giorgis, C., and Lowery, R. (2013): Books that make a difference: Kids taking action for social justice. *The Journal of Children's Literature, 39*(1), 32–35.

Tompkins, G. (2012). *Teaching writing: Balancing process and product*, (sixth edition). New York, NY: Pearson.

Van Sluys, K. (2005). *What if and why? Literacy invitations for multilingual classrooms*. Portsmouth, NH: Heinemann.

Wade, R. (2004). Citizenship for social justice. *Kappa Delta Pi Record, 40*(2), 64–68.

SOCIAL JUSTICE NONFICTION CHILDREN'S TEXTS CITED

Bridges, R. (1999). *Through my eyes*. New York, NY: Scholastic.

Hoose, P. (2009). *Claudette Colvin: Twice toward justice*. New York, NY: Farrar Straus Giroux.

Markel, M. (2013). *Brave girl: Clara and the Shirtwaist Makers' Strike of 1909* (M. Sweet, Illus.). New York, NY: Balzer + Bray/HarperCollins.

Rappaport, D. (2001). *Martin's big words: The life of Dr. Martin Luther King, Jr.* (B. Collier, Illus.). New York, NY: Scholastic.

Tonatiuh, D. (2014). *Separate is never equal: The story of Sylvia Mendez and her family*. New York, NY: Abrams Books for Young Readers.

Chapter Five

Sixth Graders' Inquiry into the World War II Japanese Internment Camps

Yoo Kyung Sung and Junko Sakoi

World War II was an important historical event worldwide. British historian John Keegan (1989) noted, "The Second World War (WWII) is the largest single event in human history, fought across six of the world's seven continents and all its oceans" (p. 5). The children's literature field in the United States mirrors this importance of WWII. The European Holocaust, Pearl Harbor, and the atomic bombings in Japan create a timeline in literary worlds. These topics are frequently revisited in relation to WWII in children's literature as children's books about Japanese internment camps (JICs).

In 1942, two months after Japan's attack on Pearl Harbor, President Franklin Roosevelt issued an executive order to create JICs. Ten of these camps were established in California, Idaho, Utah, Arizona, Wyoming, Colorado, and Arkansas (History.com, 2009). Japanese Americans were ordered to leave their homes and relocate to these remote internment camps for approximately two to four years (Nagata, Kim, & Nguyen, 2015; Takaki, 2012).

In total, 120,000 innocent men, women, and children were imprisoned in JICs without individual review or regard for their demonstrated loyalty to the United States; two-thirds were young American-born citizens (Nagata et al., 2015). The US government also arrested and imprisoned thousands of Japanese American men in Santa Fe, New Mexico, labeling them "dangerous enemy aliens" (New Mexico PBS).

The term "internment" is inaccurate and improper as it refers to "the legally permissible detention of enemy aliens in time of war" (Nagata et al., 2015, p. 356). Modern history now considers the term "incarceration" to be more accurate (Densho, n.d.). In this chapter, we refer to these locations as

JICs, because this is the most commonly known name, especially in schools. However, we suggest that teachers discuss the politics of language softening when they cover WWII units in their classrooms.

Even though some may consider WWII to be the most important war in the United States thus far, few teachers raise awareness about JICs with students. Few researchers have investigated JIC and nonfiction book practices in classrooms. In one of these investigations, Mosley (2009) carried out a book club study of Japanese internment with her second-grade class. She analyzed their critical responses to nonfiction and fiction picture book stories about Japanese Americans' lives both during and after the camp experiences, such as *The Bracelet* (Uchida & Yardley, 1993).

Mosley (2009) observed that students' conceptual understanding of power and justice grew stronger, especially regarding social and political issues between the United States and Japan. Foster (2015) conducted a historical study on elementary schools during the internment camp era in Arkansas and found currently known as "best teaching practices" were applied from 1942–1945, even though the barrack environments behind the wired wall were hard.

In this chapter, the authors share sixth graders' inquiry journey in a JIC unit. There are two sets of inquiry foci. The first inquiry details what happened in the students' new reflective learning, as they go through the "accessing, determining, and recalling" process using the Know, Want to Know, Learned (KWL) Strategy (Ogle, 1986, p. 565) within a Curriculum That Is International (CTII) framework (Short, 2009, Appendix A), which is a model for transforming beliefs into teaching practices in classrooms.

The second inquiry focuses on reflections about our practices as teacher educators. We question how we engage students with the history of JICs that might have been unfamiliar to them, and it was extra challenging when students reacted to this history as stories of others.

THE SIXTH GRADERS

The sixth graders were from a racially diverse school in Arizona. Hispanics exceed 70 percent of the school's total enrollment, followed by European Americans, African Americans, American Indians, and Asian Americans (Tucson Unified School District, 2017). Twenty-two students participated in this study: eighteen Mexican Americans (mostly second- and third-generation), one Mexican American with Japanese ancestry, one Mexican American with Native American ancestry, one European American, and one Iraqi. Mr. Gonzalez, the classroom teacher, identified as Mexican American. Yoo Kyung and Junko were participant-observers for the planning unit and leading lessons, and co-thinkers for supporting student learning and collecting and analyzing students' artifacts.

The sixth graders participated in classroom discussions and engagements, including KWL charts, written and artistic responses to texts (Graffiti Board), a poetry project, and a book author/illustrator study. An ethnography study method inspired the co-authors to keep field notes to collect the students' dialogues, anecdotes, and artifacts to uncover their learning experiences and thinking processes.

ADOPTING CURRICULUM FRAMEWORK

The decision to begin this inquiry project was based on the fact that WWII curricula in schools tend to be dominated by information about Europe or the United States. The plan originally was to challenge the US-oriented WWII perspectives by expanding to Asia. However, the students revealed that their understanding of WWII events that took place on US soil was not yet solid; the history of JICs is still relatively unavailable compared with information about other WWII events. Accordingly, the focus of the inquiry shifted.

In the beginning of the inquiry, some students showed strong interest in the researchers' ethnic backgrounds; Junko is Japanese, and Yoo Kyung is Korean. Their favorable past experiences with Japanese manga and anime or Korean pop music helped the researchers to draw their attention to Asian cultures and further JIC topics. However, a majority of the students expressed initial reluctance about JICs and learning the history of "Asians." Hapgood and Fennes (1997) noted that resistance is the very first reactionary step in recognizing intercultural learning.

In the inquiry journey, we assessed the sixth graders' current understanding of immigrants and refugees in the United States when we explained that Japanese Americans were ordered to evacuate to the West Coast but were then moved into camps. Most students viewed JICs as "their/Japanese" history instead of "our/American" history. Such indifference may mirror prevalent social attitudes of how the histories of immigrants are dealt and discussed in schools. One reason that explains the students' unfamiliarity with JICs is that historical events are selectively recognized, depending on "whose" history they are.

The southwest community environment in which these sixth graders live has common immigration public discourses, specifically for Mexican immigrants. Yet Japanese Americans are considered non-Americans by many of the sixth graders. For example, Amanda (all students' names mentioned here are pseudonyms) thought that JICs were located in Japan instead of in the United States. Students struggled to see their personal identities in the cross-cultural society in which Japanese Americans belong. As a result, we adopted

Short's (2009) CTII framework that centers personal identity in critical global discourse (see Appendix A).

Short (2009) notes that the CTII helps multiple ways of engaging with international perspectives to "support children's critical explorations of their own cultural identities, ways of living within specific global cultures, the range of cultural perspectives within any unit of study, and complex global issues" (p. 3). CTII enabled us to further challenge students' understanding of their own personal cultural identities and draw interconnectivity across personal identity and space to cross-cultural contexts in global society.

While the CTII provided a conceptual framework to lead our inquiry journey, KWL helped us design other strategies and book selections to engage the students with the JIC inquiry focus. Different types of books that support three sections in the KWL—"I know," "I want to know," and "I learned"—were selected.

WAYS TO SELECT BOOKS

In this inquiry, we aimed for students to develop confidence in reading nonfiction books. Fiction books were utilized as secondary tools to support their nonfiction book experiences. The book-selecting process focused on two aspects. First, any selected nonfiction texts had to be comprehensible by sixth graders. In addition, we exposed them to a variety of multimodal forms of nonfiction texts as well as traditional texts, such as novels, picture books, biographies, and informational books.

A biography chapter book, *Dear Miss Breed* (Oppenheim, 2006), focuses on actual survivors' stories and episodes from JICs. *Imprisoned* (Sandler, 2013) and *Uprooted* (Marrin, 2016) are chapter book–format informational books that provide detailed information of JICs and Japanese Americans' early journeys to the United States, along with rich photographic references of incarcerations and Japanese American families.

To be developmentally appropriate (to reduce the students' anxieties about these nonfiction texts), we chose a picture book biography, *Barbed Wire Baseball* (Moss & Shimizu, 2013), which appears to include the voices from the nonfiction collection. A short documentary film entitled *Remembering the Santa Fe Japanese Internment Camp* also was used as an important multimodal text.

In addition to the nonfiction texts, we selected the following historical fiction picture book and novels, *A Place Where Sunflowers Grow* (Tai & Hoshino, 2006), *A Diamond in the Desert* (Fitzmaurice, 2012), and *Gaijin* (Faulkner, 2014). KWL is a helpful activity, yet sometimes we saw a need to build the "Know" within KWL with fiction books in order to lead the nonfiction-driven inquiry journey.

Professional reviews such as Scholastic Book Reviews, Book Links, and award booklists presented by the National Council for Social Studies supported our book collecting process. We also reviewed the books and film with the classroom teacher, Mr. Gonzalez, to ensure that the contents would be appropriate and meaningful to the sixth graders. Table 5.1 provides specific book information.

LOOKING CLOSELY AT JAPANESE INTERNMENT CAMP INQUIRY AND TIMELINE

We shared nonfiction and fiction texts with the sixth graders for fourteen class sessions over a period of two months. The JIC unit was covered twice a week and each session lasted for sixty to ninety minutes. To guide the students' inquiry about the JIC history, we mapped a series of literacy engagements that would challenge them to learn in a multitude of ways. We applied mixed engagements within the KWL frame (see Appendix B), Graffiti Boards (see Appendices C and D), reading logs, journaling, and oral discussions that enriched their thought processes and responses as their readings change, and are revisited. Ogle (1986) defines KWL as a "procedure that consists with accessing what I Know, determining what I Want to learn, and recalling what I did Learn as a result of reading" (p. 565).

The first two steps (*Know* and *Want to know*) involve oral discussions followed by the students' personal responses, and then they complete the third section by reading an expository text (Ogle, 1986). These tasks helped us to engage the students in discussing, reading, reflective writing, and individual and group activities. Table 5.2 shows the details of books and relevant response activities applied in their responses within the CTII frame.

Fiction Books to Explore Personal Cultural Identities

Amy Lee-Tai's fiction picture book, *A Place Where Sunflowers Grow*, and Fitzmaurice's *A Diamond in the Desert* were shared as part of the personal identity theme of the first two sessions. The JIC topic was new to the students, so they easily fell into a familiar ritual of reading aloud, especially in reaction to the picture book, *A Place Where Sunflowers Grow*. One student (Mira) expressed that she was glad to see how Mari, the young girl protagonist, ended up drawing her family barrack with sunflowers like a new garden at the end of the story. Like Mira, many sixth graders did not catch that Mari had a critical issue. She struggled with ideas for her art assignments due to her traumatic transition (forced relocation).

After these sessions, we realized that reading aloud has to be carried out in a precise manner so that students are given adequate time and the chance to pay close attention to each illustration and narrative.

Table 5.1. Children's Books about Japanese Internment Camps

Genre	Medium	Title, Year of publication, Author/Illustrator	Annotation
Nonfiction	Picture book	*Barbed Wire Baseball: How One Man Brought Hope to the Japanese Internment Camps of WWII* (2013) by Marissa Moss and Yuko Shimizu	Kenichi Zenimura, known as a "father of Japanese American baseball," is sent to the Gila River internment camp in Arizona. There, baseball gives him and other Japanese Americans hope.
	Chapter book	*Dear Miss Breed: True Stories of the Japanese American Incarceration during World War II and a Librarian Who Made a Difference* (2006) by Joanne Oppenheim	Miss Breed, the children's librarian at the San Diego Public Library, and her incarcerated young Japanese American friends corresponded. She carries books and other treats to them.
	Chapter book	*Imprisoned: The Betrayal of Japanese Americans during World War II* (2013) by Martin W. Sandler	The time before and during imprisonment of Japanese Americans, and after their release, is presented through unpublished interviews of camp survivors.
	Chapter book	*Uprooted: The Japanese American Experience during World War II* (2016) by Albert Marrin	Pearl Harbor and Japanese internment camps are illuminated. The author gives insight into current political and social events as it does in the past.
	Film	*Remembering the Santa Fe Japanese Internment Camp* by New Mexico PBS	The Santa Fe Internment Camp is presented. There, 4,555 men of Japanese ancestry were interned as "dangerous enemy aliens."

Fiction	Picture book	*A Place Where Sunflowers Grow* (English/Japanese bilingual) (2006) by Amy Lee Tai and Felicia Hoshino	Mari, a young Japanese American girl, in the Utah's Topaz Relocation Center, misses her home in California. Drawings help her to release emotions and give her strength.
	Chapter book	*A Diamond in the Desert* (2012) by Kathryn Fitzmaurice	Tetsu's family is interned at the Gila River Internment Camp, Arizona. Baseball becomes an important thing that gives light to their deplorable life.
	Graphic novel	*Gaijin: American Prisoner of War* (2014) by Matt Faulkner	Koji's life, with a Japanese father and an American mother, is difficult with his outsider status despite his citizenship in California, and even harder in a camp as an "enemy alien."

Many words and settings in the JIC context were new to these sixth graders. Questions several raised were: "What is a barrack?" "What does internment mean?" "What is in an internment camp?" and most importantly, "Who are Japanese Americans?" This indicated that the JIC history was unknown to them.

Many students agreed that they had never heard about JICs. Thus, *A Place Where Sunflowers Grow* offered a powerful invitation for them to learn about that aspect of US history and to examine an untold point of view on Pearl Harbor from the sides of Japanese Americans. This allowed them to also raise emotive questions about Japanese Americans' feelings in these situations.

During the third through fifth sessions, students read a historical fiction novel, *A Diamond in the Desert*, independently in the classroom or at home. They had open-ended discussions in the classroom; worked on KWL charts; wrote and sketched their thoughts, ideas, connections, and questions on Graffiti Boards; and created reading logs on their own. In this novel, the story is set at the Gila River Japanese Internment Camp in Arizona, which is also the sixth graders' home state; that a JIC was in their home state was new information to them.[AQ2]

They were able to imagine life in the Gila River JIC using their own experiences with the severe hot, dry, and dusty desert life they know in Arizona. Some students made personal connections with the protagonists in the story. They drew pictures that indicated that they have lizards or iguanas as pets to keep them company much in the same way as one of the Japanese American girl characters in the novel. The decision to keep a pet or leave it

Table 5.2. Timeline in Japanese Internment Camp Unit

Sessions	Components of "A Curriculum That Is International"	Literacy Engagements with Nonfiction and Fiction Texts
1–5	Personal Cultural Identities	*A Place Where Sunflowers Grow* (fiction) • Read aloud • Open-ended discussion *A Diamond in the Desert* (fiction) • Independent reading • Graffiti Board • Know, Want to Know, Learned chart • Reading log • Open-ended discussion *Barbed Wire Baseball* (nonfiction) • Know, Want to Know, Learned chart • Graffiti Board • Reading log
6–13	Cross-Cultural Studies	*Barbed Wire Baseball*, *Dear Miss Breed*, *Imprisoned*, and *Uprooted* (nonfiction) • Know, Want to Know, Learned chart • Author and illustrator study • Reading log • Open-ended discussion Santa Fe Internment Camp film (nonfiction) • Open-ended discussion • Graffiti Board
14	Integration of International Perspectives	*Barbed Wire Baseball*, *Uprooted*, *Imprisoned*, and *Dear Miss Breed* (nonfiction) • "Where I'm From" poem

behind to relocate to a JIC made a significant impact on many of the sixth graders and allowed them to empathize with the victims.

The sixth graders displayed increased interest in Japanese American history after becoming aware of the location of the camp in Arizona and making personal connections with the victims. Other perspectives they had in the beginning of the inquiry softened, and questions soon reflected authentic curiosity about the victims' experiences in JIC: "What did they eat?" "Did they get paid?" "What were their lives like after the camps?" "Did they get their homes back?" and "How long did they stay there?"

Within CTII framework, the students showed empathetic yet cross-cultural connections. Simultaneously, the KWL chart is activated with basic questions such as, "Why did Japan attack Pearl Harbor from the beginning?" After the fiction story sessions, the focus switched to nonfiction texts to let the students notice the difference in reading fiction and nonfiction books on a topic like JICs.

Transitioning to Informational Books for Cross-Cultural Studies

For the last inquiry sessions, the sixth graders were allowed to choose nonfiction texts that interested them to learn more about JIC history. They selected paired books (*Uprooted*, *Imprisoned*, or *Dear Miss Breed*) with *Barbed Wire Baseball* to read on their own, with a partner, or in a small group. Allowing students to make this choice about their paired books encouraged them to be proactive with their exploration and to maintain the nature of an inquiry project, which enhances individual and group-oriented collaborative inquiry learning.

They read the books they felt would provide answers to their questions, such as "What were their (Japanese American) lives like after leaving the camp?" "Did the Japanese Americans get paid (in the camp)?" and "What did they eat in the camp?"

In addition, the students added what they learned and the things that they would want to know more about in KWL charts, including "What do *Nisei* and *Sansei* mean?" "Why did the US government not trust them (Japanese Americans)?" "Why did they (Japanese Americans) have to speak a different language (besides Japanese)?" "What does *patriotic* mean?" and "Why did Japan attack Pearl Harbor and China?"

They also researched authors and illustrators to identify who wrote/illustrated the JIC nonfiction texts. Authors/illustrators of interest included: Marissa Moss and Yuko Shimizu (*Barbed Wire Baseball*) and Albert Marrin, who published *Uprooted*. They read the authors' endnotes and official websites to understand their backgrounds and involvement in the creation process of these books.

The students also paid attention to the narrative voice in the stories. This author study improved their understanding of immigrants, and so it became one of the activities we added for their responsive needs.

Additional documentary video about the Santa Fe Japanese Internment Camp provided actual voices of survivors and witnesses. This further elevated their authentic response on a personal level. The Japanese interviewees' perspectives provoked them with "actuality." They cared about how it would feel to be arrested and imprisoned without clear explanations about the relocation policy.

The documentary film set the tone for authentic learning, responsive, and collaborative exploration of JICs, while pursuing aesthetic and informational responses to texts (Rosenblatt, 1994). After reading the nonfiction books, finishing the author study, and watching the film, they wrote two poems: one about the students' personal lives and identities, and another written from a Japanese American's viewpoint during the war.

Creating Poems: Developing Intercultural Perspective by Reflecting upon Personal Identity

The students wrote a poem about "Where I'm From" to locate their personal identities. This poem-writing strategy was introduced by Linda Christensen (2004). Observing the students' conceptual othering experiences in JICs urged us to invite them to make humanity connections so that it is part of "our" history not "theirs (Japanese)." The "Where I'm From" poem gave students the chance to think about the spaces and landscapes where they spent their childhoods.

In other words, they had the opportunity to describe their cultures beyond ethnicity alone. Most importantly, they reflected upon the personal values that make up part of their cultural identities in their timelines. After writing their initial personal poems, they wrote another "Where I'm From" poem in an attempt to place themselves into the same situation as Japanese Americans who were in and out of the camps during WWII.

The mixed children's books about JICs offered a range of choices from which to choose the subject of the poem. The students imagined Japanese American people's feelings, emotions, possible thoughts, and circumstances faced during the war using narratives, expository texts, and photographic images they read and revisited from nonfiction books, such as *Uprooted*, *Imprisoned*, and *Barbed Wire Baseball*.

The experience of writing these two poems enabled them to find personal connections with Japanese Americans in terms of mixed-race identity and commonality of life experiences and interests. This realization allowed them to gain in-depth insight into and a solid understanding of Japanese Americans' life experiences. They also recognize Japanese Americans as human beings beyond their racial identity.

For example, in his poem, Chapo, a second-generation Mexican American, expressed his Mexican American racial identity, the importance of Mexican meals when his family reunites, and his favorite sports and video games. Likewise, in another poem, this student wrote from the perspective of Kenichi Zenimura, the Japanese American main character in *Barbed Wire Baseball*. He conveyed the importance of Japanese and American foods for his family gatherings as well as his favorite sport (Table 5.3). The subjective stance Chapo adopted in his approach to Kenichi Zenimura's experience created an affective connection that could have emerged.

What They Learned through the Japanese Internment Camps Inquiry Journey

At the end of this inquiry journey, by following KWL strategy, students were encouraged to reflect about what they had learned about JIC history. Through whole-class discussions, focus groups, and individual interviews, they shared their views, which led us to conclude that they actually gained diverse perspectives and thoughts about the history of Japanese Americans and JICs from their readings of the nonfiction and fiction texts. In addition, they discovered that their personal life experiences resonated with the Japanese Americans' experiences during the war and enhanced their understanding of the current socio-political and global issues from a critical stance.

Multiple Perspectives through a Holistic View

Students recognized ordinary people and the government as separate units (i.e., the American people versus the American government). They mentioned positions, such as guards, teachers, and government employees, instead of "America" or "Americans." They were also aware of differences and similarities in historical tragedies, like the European Holocaust, which had been covered in the previous unit.

Several students pointed out a new perspective on the US government's incarceration of Japanese Americans other than demonizing them as spies:

Table 5.3. Situating Myself through "Where I'm From" Poem

Poem about Personal Life	Poem from Kenichi Zenimura's Perspective (Barbed Wire Baseball)
Where I'm From	Where I'm From
I'm from Tucson, Arizona	I'm from Hawaii, U.S.
My family is from Mexico	I grew up playing
Family reunion with everyone	Baseball and having
We eat all kinds of Mexican food	fun with my family
Carne Asada, Tamales, Tacos	and friends.
I like all kinds of sports	I'm from Baseball
Basketball, football, etc.	I like the New
I like Green Bay Packers	York Yankees
I like Chicago Bulls	and with family
I also like Boston Red Sox	liking playing too.
I like playing my Xbox	I'm from my
I like playing 2k 16&17	family with Japanese
I like playing madden 17	food and American
I also like playing GTA	food. Also, with
And call of duty 2 and 3	Family reunion.

> **Levi:** *(Japanese Americans) in the camps had more freedom . . . it was a "home away from home" because it was during the war and the (US) government and president didn't want the people to die in their homes, so he or she wanted them to go to the internment camps for more safety.*
> **Junko:** *The government tried to protect them?*
> **Levi:** *Yes. Like the Holocaust and (in) internment camps, they (Jewish people) were killed. (Japanese) internment camps kept them safe.*

The nonfiction books allowed students like Levi to gain additional points of view on the US government's attitude toward JICs, for though an internment camp, Japanese Americans had some freedom. They maintained ordinary day routines such as playing sports, gardening, drawing, and schooling in spite of the prevailing controlled circumstances at the internment camp. For students, it was contrasting them with Nazi concentration camps, where Jewish people were used as slave laborers and killed. In addition, they found trust and considerate relationships between some Japanese Americans and Americans while they were interned.

Karma wrote in her reading log, "I learned that she (Miss Breed) sent books to the kids in the camps. Some people volunteered to come (to the camp) and teach (Japanese American children)." Nate responded to the Santa Fe Japanese Internment Camp film by writing on his Graffiti Board, "The (American) guards (of the camp) are just laid back because they think they're (Japanese American men) not going to do anything (harm)."

Historical and Current Political Events Affecting "My" Life

Bullying and rejecting the experience of the Japanese people during WWII unfortunately continues. Kat, Nate, and Fatima shared such connectivity in their words. Kat, who was the only European American student in the class, expressed her frustration at being picked on by people at school and in her neighborhood because she was white.

> **Kat:** *I like the part where they got sent a letter, and the (Japanese American) boy is going to the camp; he started yelling, "Why am I being sent to the internment camp when my identity cannot do anything?" That is the Japanese was bombing Pearl Harbor and it's not me (the boy). . . . They (Japanese Americans) were bullied and hurt because of World War II, and it wasn't their fault at all.*
> **Junko:** *You think your situation is similar to that?*
> **Kat:** *Yeah.*

Kat expressed her struggle with her own racial identity in her community. Japanese Americans' experiences during the war powerfully validated her struggles and discomfort due to her white identity. Particular resistance and fear about the new atmosphere involved with a new government emerged through the JIC unit. Kat's statement that, "My identity cannot do anything!" showed us that the sixth graders began to understand social injustice, as the Japanese people's ethnicity was the problem, not their actions.

It was a powerful yet challenging moment to consider the power dynamic in a society where marginalization takes many different contexts, yet feelings of fear and frustration are quite similar to those experienced during the Japanese incarceration of WWII. Several students' backgrounds drew a wide range of responses.

Nate, a Mexican American boy, expressed his feelings about how the political situation now affects his own life.

> **Nate:** *How the Japanese were treated before, that's how the Mexicans are now with Trump. I didn't like Trump when he said that Mexicans are dirty, how they are rapists and they do drugs and all that. A very small number of people do those things, but now he says that all Mexicans do. That's why most Mexicans don't like him, because he says that. How everyone that was Japanese they were bad and that's how Trump is saying. How Mexicans are dirty. . . . How all the Japanese people were bad because they said all of them bombed us (Pearl Harbor).*

In addition to Nate, Fatima, who identified as Muslim and had immigrated from Iraq several years ago, addressed what has been happening to Muslims worldwide, and then stated, "Many things that were happening in the past are kind of calling back to now, and it's not good at all." These conversations helped the students recognize difficulties and struggles in their own lives and establish a common ground for viewing issues related to race, ethnicity, and religion. Past and present interests and experiences that readers bring into interactions with texts, as well as social and cultural contexts, influence their literary responses and stances (Rosenblatt, 1995).

The students' social attitudes and views based on their identities strongly yet powerfully emerged in their responses through the JIC inquiry. Their voices reminded us that personal identity in a cross-cultural context is an important component of issues in international communities. This inquiry allowed them to be honest about the issues and struggles they face, with its meaningful relevance that, indeed, touches personal identity and cross-cultural studies.

Textbox 5.1

Dear Teachers

In this Japanese internment camp history inquiry unit, we identified a pattern in which students' personal connections played a significant role in transacting with multimodal nonfiction texts. At the same time, reading and other literacy engagement activities with these texts allowed the sixth graders to participate in an active inquiry. We summarized what we learned from this unit that would be helpful for teachers as follows:

- The two genres of historical fiction and nonfiction serve two different roles. If students have minimum Knows, teachers should construct some new knowing with fiction books before nonfiction books.
- Teachers must learn to use nonfiction books as a vehicle. Equip them with nonfiction text literacy. Students often fail to realize they do not have to read nonfiction in the same manner as they read fiction, from the beginning to the end. Teachers should guide students through examples that show that readers read nonfiction books differently from fiction books.
- A range of texts should be used for reading and responding: fiction, nonfiction, and poetry ("Where I am From") to promote a new history where students see linkages across personal cultures, cross-cultural studies, and international communities and issues.
- Different types of nonfictions are required: Nonfiction books with variables help students to learn contents better (i.e., a biography, informational book, or picture book biography). Presentations of nonfiction books are important to engage students in new learning tasks.
- Multimodal supports have high effects for digital native learners. Find relevant YouTube or PBS films for your unit or guest speakers both on- and offline. We recommend *densho.org* for a Japanese internment camp unit.
- Unit connections, such as the European Holocaust, enrich other related social injustice discussions.
- Nonfiction books help our students to recognize ordinary people as different from their government. It is essential to identify the difference for their empathetic responses.
- I know better now: Students are often not well trained to (orally) talk about what they have read and discovered. They must be taught to share their new learning with others so that group discussions can be another learning opportunity. Mixed strategies that are both individual and involve group work are recommended.

CONCLUDING THOUGHTS

Teachers play a key role in fostering learning, providing psychosocial support, and establishing a sense of normality in extreme circumstances when they are passionate and dedicated (Foster, 2015). When we started this unit, we hoped JICs would be relevant to the sixth graders' lives because of the southwest connections in Arizona and New Mexico. In reality, however, their JIC knowledge was initially problematic in terms of its quality and quantity.

Because of their reluctance toward the historical event, it was challenging to draw their attention and ignite their interest. Students also had substantially narrow criteria of who Americans are, including the internally exclusive belief that minority groups were not somehow conceived as "Americans" but instead as "others." The unit aimed to change this perspective.

History becomes meaningful when students find their own stories through history and make personal connections, which are not limited to family and friends but can be applied to cultural, religious, and political landscapes, and beyond. That is how history becomes relevant to our lives and is no longer simply a subject about somebody else.

FURTHER DIRECTION

Students expanded their inquiry learning to critical issues in their global society. It is difficult to ignite new historical findings without also helping students discover their own personal identities. Our next journey is to explore unseen geography during WWII; Japan is a part of Asia, yet the power dynamics in the oppressor and the oppressed through global attacks by Japanese army and the subsequent colonization are significantly different from the JIC dynamics. We hope to investigate this using the CTII framework again, so students do not accept situations that resemble those of past Japanese Americans, but instead think of what can actually be done to make a difference.

REFERENCES

Christensen, L. (2004). Where I'm from: Inviting students' lives into the classroom. *Rethinking Our Classroom*, V.2., 6–10.

Densho. (n.d.). What both sides get wrong on "Muslim internment camps." Retrieved on May 10, 2015, from: https://www.densho.org/muslim-internment-camps/.

Fennes, H., and Hapgood, K. (1997). *Intercultural learning in the classroom: Crossing borders*. London: Cassell Council of Europe Series. Retrieved from http://www.history.com/topics/world-war-ii/japanese-american-relocation.

Foster, K. (2015). Teaching literacy behind barbed wire in WWII: Elementary schools in Japanese-American internment camps in Arkansas. *Childhood Education*, *91*(5), 378–87.

History.com. (2009). Japanese-American relocation. Retrieved from http://www.history.com/topics/world-war-ii/japanese-american-relocation.
Irons, P. (1983). *Justice at war: The story of the Japanese American internment cases*. NY: Oxford University Press.
Keegan, J. (1990). *The Second World War* (first American edition). New York: Viking.
Mosley, M. (2009). Talking about war in a second grade classroom. In R. Rogers, M. Mosley, and M. Kramer (Eds.), *Designing socially just learning communities: Critical literacy education across the lifespan*. New York: Routledge.
Nagata, D. K., Kim, J. H. J., and Nguyen, T. U. (2015). Processing cultural trauma: Intergenerational effects of the Japanese American incarceration. *Journal of Social Issues, 71*(2), 356–70.
New Mexico PBS. (June 24, 2017). Remembering the Santa Fe Japanese internment camp. Retrieved from http://www.newmexicopbs.org/moments-in-time/remembering-the-santa-fe-japanese-internment-camp/.
Ogle, D. M. (1986). K-W-L: A teaching model that develops active reading of expository texts. *The Reading Teacher, 39*(6), 564–70.
Rosenblatt, L. M. (1994). *The reader, the text, the poem: The transactional theory of the literary work*. Carbondale: Southern Illinois University Press.
Rosenblatt, L. M. (1995). *Literature as exploration*. New York: Modern Language Association of America.
Short, K. G. (2009). Critically reading the word and the world: Building intercultural understanding through literature. *Bookbird: A Journal of International Children's Literature, 47*(2), 1–10.
Takaki, R. (2012). *A different mirror for young people: A history of multicultural America*. New York: Seven Stories Press.
Tucson Unified School District. (2017). *Desegregation and Unitary Status Plan: Integrated and Racially Concentrated Schools*. Retrieved from http://tusd1.org/contents/distinfo/deseg/integrated.asp.

CHILDREN'S BOOKS CITED

Faulkner, Matt. 2014. *Gaijin: American Prisoner of War*. New York: Disney Hyperion.
Fitzmaurice, Kathryn. 2012. *A Diamond in the Desert*. London: Puffin Books.
Lee-Tai, Amy, and Hoshino, Felicia. (2006). *A Place Where Sunflowers Grow*. New York: Lee & Low Books.
Marrin, Albert. 2016. *Uprooted: The Japanese American Experience during World War II*. Canada: Knopf Books for Young Readers.
Moss, Marissa, and Yuko Shimizu. 2013. *Barbed Wire Baseball: How One Man Brought Hope to the Japanese Internment Camps of WWII*. New York: Abrams.
Oppenheim, Joanne. 2006. *Dear Miss Breed: True Stories of the Japanese American Incarceration during WWII and a Librarian Who Made a Difference*. New York: Scholastic.
Sandler, Martin W. 2013. *Imprisoned: The Betrayal of Japanese Americans during World War II*. New York: Walker Books for Young Readers.
Uchida, Yoshiko, and Yardley, Joanna. 1993. *The Bracelet*. New York: Philomel.

Chapter Six

Critical Conversations Using Native American Autobiographies

Paul H. Ricks

> I have a theory that the most interesting autobiographies are the ones written by second-tier people. I'm not looking at second-tier in the derogatory sense, like second-rate. I mean it in a sense of hierarchy. When the people on the top tier tell their story, it's invariably boring. They have too much to lose by being honest. Their public stature works against them on the page because they know anything they write that's even vaguely controversial or opinionated—in other words, anything interesting—it's going to get dissected and distorted by the media. But the memoir of the person *under* the general, or the president, or the CEO—the person you've never heard of—that person has a lot less to lose, and their memoirs are where the gold lies.
> —Gladwell, 2017, n.p.

Though Gladwell speaks of autobiography broadly, the above quote can apply specifically to reasons educators will wish to use Native American autobiographical texts in their classrooms. Historically, Native American voices have not been privileged in literature for young readers, with nonfiction not being the exception (Bradford, 2007; MacCann, 1992; Reese and Caldwell-Wood, 1998).

Authors of nonfiction tend to concentrate on a handful of mythologized and fetishized Native American figures (e.g., Sacagawea, Pocahontas, Geronimo, Squanto) in biographical accounts that are often "inaccurate, inauthentic, patronizing, full of lies, and altogether a huge insult to the people out of whose lives so much money is being made" (Seale, 2005, p. 4). The autobiography, however, offers spaces for people to tell their own stories. For Native Americans whose voices have long been marginalized in mainstream literature for young readers, the autobiography can provide "the unique viewpoint of self-revelation" (Tunnell, Jacobs, Young, and Bryan, 2016, p. 171) that helps to counter many of the insidious falsehoods created in large part by outsider voices and perspectives.

In the twenty-first century, the vast majority of books written about Native American people continue to be written by non-Native authors (Crosetto and Garcha, 2013). Literature that is written *about* rather than *by* Native Americans often presents stories that objectify by silencing and dehumanizing the "other," and which provide mediated and limited understanding because of cultural insights and considerations that often elude the authors.

Bruchac (2011) reminds us that,

> Culture, like language is very specific. If you do not learn it well, then you end up speaking pidgin at best and either nonsense or insult at worst. That is why, to put it plainly, the vast majority of books for kids "about" so-called indigenous cultures that have been written by white people are stupid or insensitive. (p. 342)

Three autobiographical texts—*Saltypie: A Choctaw Journey from Darkness into Light* (Tingle, 2010), *Fatty Legs: A True Story* (Jordan-Fenton and Pokiak-Fenton, 2010), and *Looks Like Daylight: Voices of Indigenous Kids* (Ellis, 2013)—are refreshing departures from the "top-tier" stories penned by those who "have too much to lose by being honest" (Gladwell, 2017, n.p.). For teachers who agree with Botelho and Rudman (2009) that "[t]he teaching of literature should begin with social justice" (p. 268), these texts provide opportunities for rich discussions and critical engagement, as they focus on sociopolitical topics often avoided in children's literature.

As readers, ours is the great privilege of accessing stories that are "a portal through which a person enters the world and by which their experience of the world is interpreted and made personally meaningful" (Connelly and Clandinin, 2006, p. 477). This chapter offers critical readings of autobiographical texts that unapologetically provide the "gold" (Gladwell, 2017, n.p.) for conversations about race and racism, ways of dealing with injustice, and the complex histories that inform and influence the present-day lives of Native American people.

PREPARING TO ACTIVELY APPROACH AUTOBIOGRAPHICAL TEXTS

It has been my experience that many educators are unsure of where to start when it comes to having critical conversations in their own classrooms. They are often looking for an entry point—they want to engage in discussions that go beyond the sanitized, surface-level readings that happen in school settings—but certain questions remain: Is it my place to take a stance on sociopolitical issues? Shouldn't I try to be more objective? Am I really the right person for this? What if I say the wrong thing?

Educators who wish to engage in critical conversations with their students must lead by example. They may question their expertise on topics such as race, class, gender, and myriad defining characteristics of specific cultural groups, but they must also recognize that a lack of experience or understanding is not an insurmountable stumbling block.

In an effort to advocate for respectful representation, well-intentioned educators can take meaningful first steps by turning to nonfiction as a means of providing additional insight and clarity when discussing unfamiliar or sensitive topics. Autobiographical texts written by cultural insiders can be particularly valuable, as they often present authoritative narratives that counter those of the dominant culture.

Teachers must remember, however, that to lead their students they must take up what Botelho and Rudman (2009) refer to as an *active* stance toward a text. Readers who take an active stance will not simply accept "the authors' words and illustrators' images unquestioningly" (2009, p. 267); rather, they will engage with the text critically by reading beyond the "explicit messages of the author and/or illustrator" (p. 267). Autobiographical texts written by cultural insiders are only fertile grounds for exploration and inquiry insomuch as they are questioned and critiqued.

Though it may well be readers' "birth right to be active producers of meaning" (Gee, 2014, p. xii), pithy conversations and critical engagement will not happen through minimal effort or passive acceptance of everything presented on the page.

In an effort to encourage teachers who want to engage in critical conversations but who are unsure of where to start, the remainder of this chapter offers analyses of autobiographical texts that present topics and subject matter (e.g., hate crimes toward Native Americans, abuse in off-reservation boarding schools, isolation from family and culture through loss of language and traditions) that open spaces for such discussions.

Each analysis is divided into three parts—reading *with* the text and its overt messages, strategies for further engagement, and reading *against* the text through an active stance of interpretation—to show how well-written, insightful, and informative narratives can also be questioned, critiqued, and reconsidered.

Chapter 6

CRITICAL READING OF
SALTYPIE: A CHOCTAW JOURNEY FROM DARKNESS INTO LIGHT

This picture book biography tells the story of how the author's family came to use the neologism "saltypie." The phrase originated from a violent assault in which the author's grandmother, standing in the doorway to meet the new dawn, was cut across the face when an unknown boy threw a stone at her because she was Native American.

When the author's father, just two years old at the time, saw his mother bleeding and holding her face in her hands, he licked between her fingers because he thought the blood was cherry pie filling. Shocked by the taste, he screamed, "Saltypie!" which in turn became the phrase his family used to deal with and describe certain of life's difficulties and injustices, especially those without simple solutions.

Reading with the Text

Part of the power of this story is that the author and illustrator unflinchingly show scenes not typically found in nonfiction picture books for young readers. When the author's grandmother stumbles into the house after being hit with a stone, a two-page spread is shown in which she holds her bloody face in her hands. The image helps readers to see and understand the horrific effects of violence and hatred.

For those who wonder whether such gritty portrayals should be included in a book for children, the author defends the depictions of real-life violence in a three-page section entitled "How Much Can We Tell Them?" Tingle states that "[m]any non-Indian people have difficulty believing that bigotry could still be alive, or could ever have been alive, in the settling of our nation, in our dealings with Indians" (n.p.). By "revealing previously hidden truths" (n.p.) in a straightforward manner, the author and illustrator help young readers to face the wrongs of the past and encourage all to become agents of change who "leave happy footfalls behind us in our going" (n.p.).

Saltypie: A Choctaw Journey from Darkness into Light can also be useful in encouraging critical outlooks because of its representations of present-day Native Americans. Reese and Caldwell-Wood (1998) state that "the greatest need . . . is for more books that provide a contemporary perspective of Native American people, particularly Native American children" (p. 181) because of the false notion that persists among young readers that Native Americans existed exclusively in the distant past and that they have no place in the modern world.

Perhaps countering certain readers' expectations, the author and illustrator present characters whose homes, clothing, and occupations differ greatly from the stereotypical teepees, loincloths, and hunter-gatherer lifestyles so often found in other children's literature texts.

Strategy for an Active Stance: Same Facts, Different Stories

Purpose: To demonstrate that even if we see the same thing, we talk about it in our own ways

Prepare students by telling them you are going to light some money on fire and that they are going to write about what happens. This should get their attention. Mix three parts rubbing alcohol with one part water in a cup. Dip a dollar bill in the solution using metal tongs, and then light the bill on fire (still holding it with the tongs) using a match or a lighter. Because of the water in the alcohol-water solution, the bill will light on fire, but it will only burn for a few seconds before the entire bill dries, leaving it completely unharmed.

Then ask students to write about what happened in three to five sentences. After each person has written a short paragraph, have a few students read their responses aloud to the class. As they do, make sure that students notice the similarities and differences between the various accounts. Was there something one wrote about that another did not? What about the way it was described? Was everything told in the same order and timeline? Were some descriptions more succinct while others were more detailed? How could that happen if everyone saw essentially the same thing?

Also, remind students that some responses might appear to be very similar initially, but when analyzed by word choice, tone, etc., each response is quite unique. As the activity winds down, ask students to look at their own papers and think about how their versions compare to those that have been shared. Each will be its own version of the "truth," just like the autobiographical accounts written by published authors.

Reading against the Text

How would *Saltypie: A Choctaw Journey from Darkness into Light* change if it were written by someone else? What might be different, for example, if Tingle's grandmother told the story in her own words? How would she describe the rock-throwing incident? Or what might the effects be if Tingle's grandfather, whom we are told wanted to deal with the perpetrator personally, wrote from his perspective? Though perhaps difficult to imagine, how would the story change if the boy who threw the stone were telling it?

Questions such as these can guide readers toward critical conversations, because they demonstrate how subjective one's perceptions and realities are. Tingle presents a real-life story in a way that is powerful and thought provok-

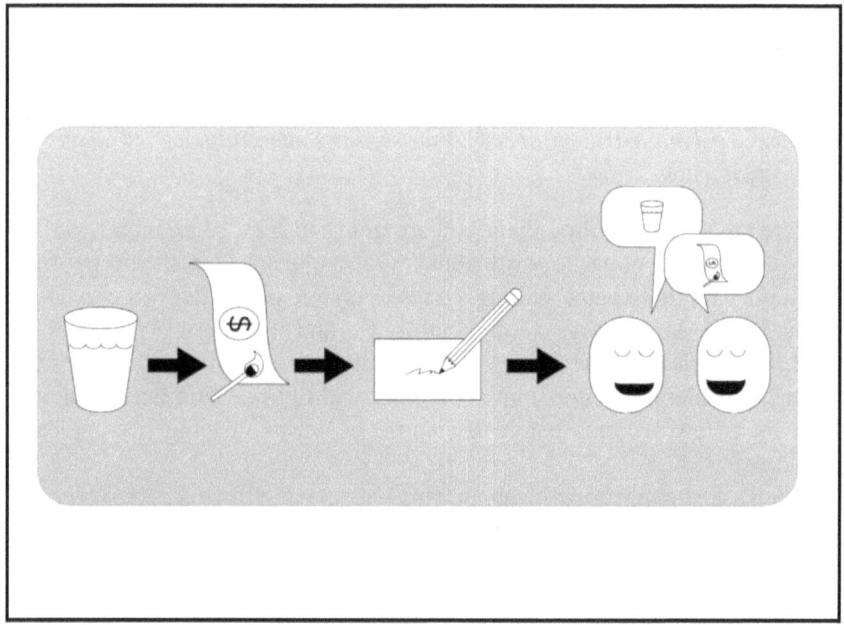

Figure 6.1. Same Facts, Different Stories.

ing, but readers must recognize that the author's truth is relative, and that his way of telling the story is not the *only* way that the story could have been told.

Readers can also ask what the story would be like if it were illustrated differently. Clarkson's decisions—from stylistic preferences to media choices to color schemes to the ways she frames and composes images—all affect how the story unfolds in the readers' minds. In one two-page spread, for example, Clarkson chooses not to show the face of the boy who threw the stone, and instead she places him next to a tree that obstructs his face from view.

Readers should be encouraged to ask what effect that has on them. Does the exclusion make one concentrate on the violent act itself rather than on the person throwing the stone? Is the effect perhaps the opposite, with the reader wondering so much who the boy is and what he looks like that the horrific act takes a backseat? Or are the effects something else entirely? Such questions help readers to recognize the subjective nature of the visual information they are presented, and that just like an author's words, an illustrator's interpretation need not be the *only* way of envisioning the images.

CRITICAL READINGS OF
FATTY LEGS: A TRUE STORY

This co-authored memoir relates an eight-year-old girl's harrowing experiences at a Catholic boarding school for Indigenous children. Despite her parents' bleak depictions and warnings of what often happens in the boarding school setting, Olemaun desperately wants to attend so that she can learn to read. She innocently assumes that her strong work ethic will allow her to avoid the traumas her parents describe, but Olemaun quickly learns that no amount of effort on her part will save her from prejudicial mistreatment.

She is physically and verbally abused, forced to take a Christian name (Margaret), required to perform grueling physical labor, surrounded by foreign diseases in the infirmary, and forbidden to speak in any language other than English. Additionally, because of a run-in she has early on with the Raven—a nun with a hooked nose and claw-like fingers—she is given ill-fitting clothes that make her the go-to target for derision from her peers, who call her "Fatty Legs." After two heartbreaking years away with essentially no correspondence of any kind, she returns to her home—able to read, but feeling like a stranger among her own family.

Reading with the Text

As outrageous as it may seem, Indian boarding schools were intentionally created "to remove children from their families at an early age and thereby isolate them from the language and customs of their parents and tribes" (Spring, 2013, pp. 32–33). Many believed that forced assimilation would "civilize" young, impressionable Native children, who in time would be cleansed of their "heathenistic" traditions and "backward" ways of living. This church- and state-enforced cleansing, however, was most often unconscionably cruel, and those who endured the hardships of residential boarding schools are more appropriately recognized as survivors, rather than mere attendees or alumni.

Fatty Legs: A True Story provides an intimate look at Pokiak-Fenton's experiences in a residential school, but her story can lead to larger conversations that deal with the centuries of subjugation and colonialization of Native people in North America. Her firsthand account uncovers many topics that have historically been glossed over or hidden from young readers, and the subject matter itself provides ample opportunity for critical engagement.

Readers will perhaps be shocked and/or enraged to hear, for example, that many children were "forcibly taken" with "some even kidnapped" because "the schools were paid a fee for each child attending" (Jordan-Fenton and Pokiak-Fenton, 2010, p. 86). As readers are exposed to the authors' matter-of-fact descriptions of the horrors inflicted on Native people, they can engage in more informed conversations that address and grapple with the complexity of history and how it is told.

Strategy for an Active Stance: Answer My Question with a Question

Purpose—To read against a text and ask questions, even if many questions remain unanswered

To begin, a student turns to someone else in a small group and asks a question. It could be something like, "Did you eat breakfast this morning?" or "How tall are you?" or even "What's your name?" The student who receives the question will then ask her or his own question to another student in the group, but they cannot answer the question asked previously, and they cannot ask the same question twice.

Only interrogative sentences are acceptable in this setting, and it is usually more effective/fun if students try to do this very quickly, as it is almost impossible to keep going for very long without making a mistake.

Then, teachers can talk to students about how a similar approach can be used to critically examine texts. Students can question anything and everything—the author, the illustrator, the photographer, the major and minor characters, publishers, etc.—but they must also realize that asking questions often leads to new questions, and it does not necessarily provide answers. Readers who ask questions will move away from having relatively passive interactions with texts, and instead they will find that critical engagement can be as simple as asking—and as complex as trying to answer—"Why did the author write this story in the first place?"

Reading against the Text

Why did Olemaun feel it was so important to learn to read in English? Would she say it was worth learning to read, considering the prices she had to pay? And what of her parents? Was it wrong of them to send their daughter away to boarding school knowing what would probably happen to her? How much did her parents really know? What were some of the long-lasting effects of Olemaun's experiences at school, both good and bad? How much did she eventually tell her family?

Was the writing of *Fatty Legs: A True Story* in some ways therapeutic? Was it painful? Perhaps both? Why was a memoir telling one person's experiences co-authored? How did having multiple authors change the way the story was told? How does Olemaun's story compare to those of other residential school survivors? What can be learned from reading such accounts?

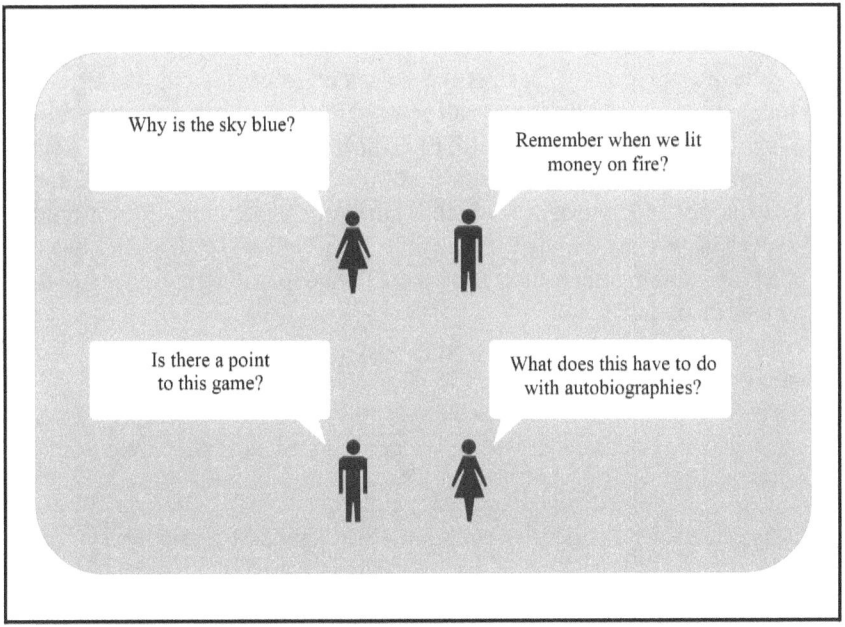

Figure 6.2. Answer my question with a question.

It is important to note that readers' questions and understandings will be influenced by many factors, not the least of which being their insider/outsider statuses and their familiarity with topics such as residential boarding schools and the abuses suffered in those settings. Bradford (2011) asserts that texts written by cultural insiders can "present challenges to readers unfamiliar with the cultures in which they are located" (p. 332), and that cultural outsiders will at times find it difficult to fully understand a text.

While in no way denying the role that cultural background plays in one's interpretation of a text, I would contend that full understanding of a text is all but impossible for cultural insiders and outsiders alike, and that all texts can challenge readers, though perhaps in different ways. That said, if readers are allowed to ask their questions openly, there will be opportunities for both collective and individual growth, as each question has the potential to direct and redirect readers toward conversations they would not have in isolation.

CRITICAL READINGS OF *LOOKS LIKE DAYLIGHT: VOICES OF INDIGENOUS KIDS*

This collective biography features the voices of forty-five Native American and Indigenous young adults from all across North America. Long the collector of stories from around the world, Ellis introduces readers to Native youths whose straightforward, first-person accounts highlight their dreams, ambitions, struggles, and hardships. Each contributor's story provides a unique and powerful witness of what it means to be a Native youth in the twenty-first century, and together, their stories create a depiction that is greater than the sum of its parts.

Reading with the Text

> It wouldn't be that hard for me—or any of us—to live now as we lived four hundred years ago. —Cohen, age fourteen

> White people are ignorant about us because they never have to think about us. They don't know what we've been through ever since the settlers came. —Destiny, age fifteen

> Naming ceremonies are sacred. They mean something. I don't think the teacher understood that. —Isabella, age fourteen

> I'm more Ojibwe than American. —Cuay, age twelve

Looks Like Daylight: Voices of Indigenous Kids is a far-reaching departure from children's and young adult literature norms, because it privileges the thoughts and opinions of the voices most often silenced in texts for young readers—those of actual young people. As the above quotes demonstrate, the interviewees seem to have no difficulty sharing their views on issues that often take on "safe" and/or "politically correct" wording when presented by adults, and their frank descriptions are a healthy indictment of such guarded discussions.

Educators can use the multiple perspectives presented in the text to counter the notion that all Native American and Indigenous people can be somehow reduced to any monocultural archetype. With forty-five interviewees giving nuanced descriptions of their lived experiences, readers can grow in their appreciation and understanding of the differences that define the 565 federally recognized tribes of the United States and the over six hundred First Nations communities represented in Canada.

Whether seen as mirrors, windows, or sliding glass doors (Bishop, 1990), the perspectives shared in *Looks Like Daylight: Voices of Indigenous Kids* can contribute to readers' critical understandings of diversity within Native communities in North America.

Strategy for an Active Stance: Who Is This for and What Does It Do?

Purpose: To consider imagined audiences, authorial agendas, and personal responses to texts

Bring in a coin and ask, "What is this for?" Students will probably say something like, "To buy things." There will, of course, be other responses, which is the whole point. After the initial question, follow up by asking, "Can it (the coin) be used in other ways, and if so, by whom?" Students might respond that it can be flipped by a referee, such as when it is used to decide which team receives the kickoff at the beginning of a football game.

Another response is that it can be made to disappear, like when a magician performs a trick. Yet another might be that it can be flicked and spun across a flat surface. The responses really are limitless. Eventually the responses will slow down, and at this point teachers can wrap things up by asking, "And how would *you* use this coin?" The purpose of this last question is to help students recognize that everything has an intended purpose (in this case, a uniform monetary system allowing one to buy and sell goods), but it can also be used and viewed in other ways, which are not necessarily wrong or less important.

Then, transition to show how the activity applies to reading. Authors write with certain audiences in mind, and critical readers can ask questions similar to those used for the coin: Who is this book for, and what does it do? As educators and students engage with these types of questions (e.g., "Who do you think the author was writing for?" "What do you think the author was trying to accomplish with this book?" "Do you think someone else might interpret this book differently than you, and if so, why?"), they can have meaningful discussions about implied audiences and authors' and/or illustrators' intentions and agendas.

This type of dialogue can help readers to critically consider how and why texts are produced, and it also helps readers to see that authors and illustrators need not be viewed as infallible beings who should be trusted for their impeccable objectivity and/or expertise.

Reading against the Text

The subtitle *Voices of Indigenous Kids*, while not incorrect, is incomplete. From brief introductions accompanying interviewees' responses to the questions asked to elicit them, Ellis's voice and influence should not be over-

> **Latex glove**—hand protectant; fill it with air and it becomes a balloon; draw two dots and a line on said balloon and it becomes a face with spikey hair
>
> **Blank sheet of paper**—backdrop for notetaking and drawing; fold a few times and it becomes an origami object; dip in flour and water and it becomes papier-mâché
>
> **Wine glass**—receptacle for liquid; musical instrument when finger is moved in a circle around the edge; dump the liquid out, fill with some coffee beans, and it becomes a pencil holder

Figure 6.3. Other Objects to See and Use "Other" Ways.

looked. Readers who ask, "Who is this text for, and what does it do?" may come to find that they disagree with certain of the ways Ellis chooses to frame her participants and their lives. For example, Ellis (2013) states that attendees of a particular boarding school "must choose between being with their families and being educated" (p. 155). Such framing might imply to some readers that the only education that "counts" is the type received in schools, thereby negating the learning that happens at home.

Additionally, many of the interviewees seem to concentrate on traumas such as teenage suicide, sexual abuse, addiction, and depression. Critical readers will ask why. Ellis (2013) states that she has "been able to meet with kids around the world whose lives have been turned upside down by people with money, power and education who ought to know better," but that she is hopeful "that everyone who reads this book will come away with a better understanding of the tremendous wealth of talent these eloquent young people can bring to the world" (p. 17).

Perhaps by encouraging Native youths to concentrate on the more traumatic events of their lives, Ellis unintentionally adopts a savior-like mentality toward her participants that can come across as condescending and even patronizing. Such readings, however, are in no way meant to vilify or condemn; rather, they show that what a text "does" for some readers may be very different from what the author originally intended.

CONCLUSION

Autobiographical texts that feature Native Americans can be invaluable resources for educators who wish to engage in critical conversations with young readers. Their long-silenced, "second-tier" (Gladwell, 2017) voices can help to make plain many of the perspectives and realities so often neglected in other children's literature texts. That said, educators do a great disservice if they "hide" behind such texts and deferentially accept everything in them. As readers take a more active stance—reading with and against the texts—they take crucial steps toward seeing and understanding the world in new ways. The "gold" is there for the taking, but we still have to dig for it.

REFERENCES

Bishop, R. (1990). Mirrors, windows, and sliding glass doors. *Perspectives, 1*(3), ix–xi.
Botelho, M. J., and Rudman, M. K. (2009). *Critical multicultural analysis of children's literature: Mirrors, windows and doors.* New York, NY: Routledge.
Bradford, C. (2007). *Unsettling narratives: Postcolonial readings of children's literature.* Waterloo, ON: Wilfrid Laurier UP.
Bradford, C. (2011). Reading indigeneity: The ethics of interpretation and representation. In S. Wolf, K. Coats, P. Enciso, and C. Jenkins (Eds.), *Handbook of research on children's and young adult literature* (pp. 331–42). New York, NY: Routledge.
Bruchac, J. (2011). Point of departure. In S. Wolf, K. Coats, P. Enciso, and C. Jenkins (Eds.). *Handbook of research on children's and young adult literature* (pp. 342–44). New York, NY: Routledge.
Connelly, F. M., and Clandinin, D. J. (2006). Narrative inquiry. In J. L. Green, G. Camilli, and P. Elmore (Eds.), *Handbook of complementary methods in education research* (third edition, pp. 477–87). Mahwah, NJ: Lawrence Erlbaum.
Crosetto, A., and Garcha, R. (2013). *Native North Americans in literature for youth: A selective annotated bibliography for K-12.* Lanham, MD: The Scarecrow.
Gee, J. (2014). Foreword. F. *Serafini, Reading the visual: An introduction to teaching multimodal literacy* (pp. xi–xii). New York, NY: Teachers College.
Gladwell, M. (Presenter). (2017, June 22). *The road to Damascus* [Audio podcast]. In M. Lobel (Producer), *Revisionist history*. Retrieved from http://itunes.apple.com/.
MacCann, D. (1992). Native Americans in books for the young. In V. Harris (Ed.). *Teaching multicultural literature in grades K-8* (pp. 137–69). Norwood, MA: Cristopher-Gordon.
Reese, D., and Caldwell-Wood, N. (1998). Native Americans in children's literature. In V. Harris (Ed.), *Using multiethnic literature in the K-8 classroom* (pp. 155–92). Norwood, MA: Cristopher-Gordon.
Seale, D. (2005). Introduction. In D. Seale and B. Slapin (Eds.). *A broken flute: The Native experience in books for children.* Walnut Creek: CA: Altamira.
Spring, J. (2013). *Deculturalization and the struggle for equality: A brief history of dominated cultures in the United States* (seventh edition). New York, NY: McGraw-Hill.
Tunnell, M. O., Jacobs, J. S., Young, T. A., and Bryan, G. (2016). *Children's literature, briefly* (sixth edition). Boston, MA: Pearson.

TRADE BOOKS CITED

Ellis, D. (2013). *Looks like daylight: Voices of Indigenous kids.* Toronto, ON: Groundwood Books/House of Anansi.
Jordan-Fenton, C., and Pokiak-Fenton, M. (2010). *Fatty Legs: A true story.* Toronto, ON: Annik.
Tingle, T. (2010). *Saltypie: A Chocktaw journey from darkness into light.* El Paso, TX: Cinco Puntos.

Chapter Seven

Biographies as Bibliotherapy

*Using Nonfiction to Help
Boys Overcome Bullying*

Lunetta M. Williams and Kelly C. Scott

Social justice includes action, especially from educators who play a pivotal role in forming the future, to reduce inequity and oppression. For the purposes of this chapter, we focus on oppression that has stemmed from bullying, a social issue that cannot be ignored among children and adolescents and defined as abusive patterns of aggression in social relationships with an imbalance of power (Olweus, 1991).

Bullying often begins as early as preschool, when children engage in name calling, threatening others with harm, creating rumors, kicking or spitting on someone, and purposefully excluding others from activities (US Department of Education, 2016). Research findings indicate that children being bullied often report low self-esteem, loneliness, and depression and are at risk of social, emotional, behavioral, and medical problems (Gini and Pozzoli, 2009).

There is a significant negative association between children who are victimized by bullies and academic achievement (Nakamoto and Schwartz, 2009), and Sourander and colleagues report that frequent victimization relates to long-term consequences in adulthood, including criminality (2007). In this chapter, we focus on boys who are bullied, as they are likely to be at excessive risk for short- and long-term academic and social consequences.

Research reveals an achievement gap between genders, even without considering bully victimization. Girls have outperformed boys on reading achievement scores for decades, especially those from low socioeconomic backgrounds (National Center for Education Statistics, 2015). Also, Brozo

(2006) notes that, overwhelmingly, boys are placed into remedial reading programs. Even at an early age and without considering the effects of being bullied, boys are overrepresented in prisons and other criminal behavior institutions (Sickmund, Sladky, Kang, and Puzzanchera, 2015).

We provide a review of literature focused on how role models and bibliotherapy support boys as they try to overcome social issues such as bullying. Using guidance from research on the decisions behind boys' selections of books and role models, we reveal three categories of role models and provide examples of related biographies. In addition to providing descriptions of the biographies, we offer suggestions about how they can be used in the classroom to help boys make themselves ready to cope with bully victimization.

Banks and colleagues noted that students must develop knowledge and skills necessary to interact with diverse people, including those who are oppressive, and participate in the nation's civic life (2001). The books and suggestions in this chapter serve to contribute to the development of these knowledge and skills.

THE INFLUENCE OF ROLE MODELS IN BIBLIOTHERAPY

Bibliotherapy is a technique that educators can use to help children heal from and develop effective coping skills after experiencing trauma such as bully victimization. While there are various ways to conduct bibliotherapy, the process typically includes reading aloud a text that is purposefully matched with students' needs and facilitating discussion that encourages students to make connections with one or more characters as well as evaluate and modify their own behaviors and emotions (De Vries, Brennan, Lankin, Morse, Rix, and Beck, 2017). The characters in bibliotherapy books offer readers "positive images of who they are and who they can become" (Zambo, 2007, p. 124).

While many texts used in bibliotherapy are fictional pieces, such as ones demonstrating how characters successfully interacted with bullies (e.g., *Your Move*, 1998, by Eve Bunting), nonfiction pieces can also be used, such as biographies. "People need role-models and idols. They offer help and orientation, for children and adolescents in particular" (Biskup and Pfister, 1999, p. 199). We assert that boys need "real" role models: humans who have encountered bullies and successfully navigated interactions with them.

Providing boys with biographies of both males and females is ideal. For example, *Heroes for My Son* (Meltzer, 2010) and *28 Days: Moments in Black History That Changed the World* (Smith Jr. and Evans, 2015) include male and female role models for children who are victimized by bullying.

In this chapter, we provide examples of biographies of male role models to further narrow the focus since previous research indicates that males tend to prefer to learn from male role models more than females (Estrada, Garcia-Ael, and Martorell, 2015; Holub, Tisak, and Mullins, 2008). Educators can provide access to or read aloud biographies about male role models as a beginning point to hook boys into wanting to learn from this genre, and biographies of females can be introduced soon thereafter.

SELECTING BIOGRAPHIES: OUR MODEL FOR FINDING ROLE MODELS IN THE LITERATURE

As we selected examples of biographies featuring male role models, we used one of Marilyn Price-Mitchell's (2015) studied qualities of a role model: someone who shows the ability to overcome obstacles, such as being bullied, as a driving definition. Recognizing there were more biographies of male role models than could fit in this chapter, we used criteria including awards earned, boys' interests, accessibility, physical characteristics, and past and present examples.

Recently published biographies that won children's book awards for nonfiction, such as the Orbis Pictus Award for Outstanding Nonfiction and Robert F. Sibert Informational Book Medal, were sought when creating a list of examples of male role models who overcame the social issue of being victims of bullies. An example of one of these award-winning books is *A Splash of Red: The Life and Art of Horace Pippin* (Bryant, 2013), which contains key events in the astounding life of Pippin as well as colorful, appealing illustrations.

We also looked at recipients of the Nobel Peace Prize and awards focused on athletes, including the Nike Casey Martin Award and National Football League (NFL) Man of the Year Award. Athlete awards were considered due to research indicating that many boys are interested in sports (Barry, 2013).

To further guide the search, we examined accessibility, making sure that the biographies could likely be found in a library, bookstore, or online. If books were accessible, we noted the book's physical characteristics, such as having an appealing cover and quality illustrations and organization (Senn, 2012).

Based on the biographies found from a search of the literature, we narrowed the examples to focus on three categories: presidents, male athletes, and males with physical challenges. For each category, we selected books that provided a past or deceased and a present, living example. Further, the books mention how the males encountered the social issue of bullying.

RECOMMENDED BIOGRAPHIES AND THE BIOS BEHIND THE BIOGRAPHIES

In this section, recommendations for biographies focused on presidents, male athletes, and males with physical challenges are described, including the rationale for why the book was selected and a teachable moment, which can be used during bibliotherapy and opportunities to discuss social justice in the classroom.

Presidents

Male participants in one study noted that important character traits for a role model included bravery and kindness (Bricheno and Thornton, 2007). Some presidents may serve as role models with these traits and ideally demonstrate them over the course of several years. The biographies of two presidents mentioned below include examples of how they demonstrated bravery and kindness to bullies.

Who Is Barack Obama? (2012) by Roberta Edwards is part of the *Who Was* and *Who Is* series, which contain short chapters and timelines of pivotal moments, serving as good introductory texts of popular people. In *Who Is Barack Obama?* readers learn about critical events in the first United States' African American president's life, such as growing up in Hawaii and Jakarta, developing a strong work ethic, starting a family, and serving in various government positions that eventually led him to becoming the forty-fourth president of the United States.

This biography mentions the time when Obama encountered bullies on the first day of attending an elementary school where peers laughed at his name, clothes, and lack of wealth. Even though Obama's stepfather taught him to box so that he could "stand up for himself," Obama attempted to fit in and find friends. By the time he was a teenager, he was well liked by his peers. Teachers could use this portion of the book as a teachable moment.

Students could discuss how Obama demonstrated bravery to find new friends as well as specific coping skills that he might have used when victimized by bullies. Also, students could share communication techniques that they have found beneficial or would like to try in the future to cope with bullies and form healthy friendships.

Beyond being bullied, this biography includes other challenges that Obama endured, such as his father's dim presence and losing an election in 2000. Also included is the fact that Obama maintained a calm, bold leadership style as he showed kindness to poor people and spoke out against war in Afghanistan. The biography's timeline mentions that Obama was awarded the Nobel Peace Prize in 2009. Students could further research why Obama won this prestigious award, as it gives further credence to why he serves as an excellent role model.

Another book that focuses on the life of a president is Meltzer and Eliopoulos's *I Am Abraham Lincoln* (2014). This biographical narrative, written in first-person, begins with Lincoln as a ten-year-old child and describes how he encountered and overcame bullies throughout his life, an aspect of his story not always mentioned in biographical accounts.

Lincoln's different encounters with bullies are described through the book's narrative text and comic-like illustrations. Examples of bullying and bravery, such as when Lincoln, at the age of ten, felt the need to speak up after witnessing other kids torturing turtles, were accompanied by Lincoln's learned lessons from the experience: "Sometimes, the hardest fights don't reveal a winner—but they do reveal character. Especially when you're fighting for something you believe in" (Meltzer, 2014, p. 20).

The situations presented of Lincoln coping with bullies at an early age can help younger nonfiction readers relate to the text and see themselves in this past president. These little-known details of Lincoln's early years can be used by teachers to provide context of his character when teaching about how Lincoln took a stand against slavery in his adult life, and how he demonstrated kindness to others. They can also be used to teach the importance of students using their voices to stand up for themselves and others.

Male Athletes

When exploring nonfiction topics that interest boys, sports-related books soar to the top (Allington, McGill-Franzen, Camilli, Williams, Graff, Zeig, Zmach, and Nowak, 2010; Barry, 2013; Williams, 2008). For this reason, male athletes were the second category of biographies we focused on in this chapter. Knowing there are many athletes who are highly visible and looked up to by young males, there is an opportunity for educators to capitalize on boys' interests when highlighting athletes who have overcome adversity and are champions for justice now and throughout history.

In *Meet Eli Manning: Football's Unstoppable Quarterback* (2009), MacRae focuses on the New York Giants' quiet, talented quarterback. Readers learn about Eli Manning's upbringing, college successes, struggles, and accomplishments as a New York Giants quarterback, as well as his contributions to society, such as working with the Red Cross to help ill children.

Several portions of the book mention Manning's experiences of being bullied. For example, fans and the media were skeptical of Manning's success because they could not envision him being as skilled as his brother, Peyton. During Manning's early years as the Giants' quarterback, his inconsistency as a player made fans so angry that they said mean things about him and boisterously booed in football stadiums. One sportswriter even jeered that Manning must be adopted. In 2007, when the Giants won the Super Bowl, Manning was named Most Valuable Player, and the biography states that this accomplishment finally silenced Manning's critics.

An activity that couples with this book is sharing a new NFL initiative, the Character Playbook, a digital course that schools can participate in for free (http://www.characterplaybook.com). Large donations were provided to this initiative in Manning's name after he was awarded the NFL Man of the Year (Eisen, 2017). Overall, the Character Playbook strives to help children develop healthy relationships and character using modules focused on topics such as communicating effectively and resolving conflicts.

Another book that highlights male athletes who are role models to young boys is *28 Days: Moments in Black History That Changed the World*, a compilation of short biographies featuring African Americans behind twenty-eight moments that changed the world between 1770 and today. Each of the twenty-eight moments, corresponding with one of the days during Black History Month, is given its own illustrated page with text in a unique format (e.g., poem or quotation) and is accompanied by related facts.

Perennial names of Black History Month, such as Martin Luther King Jr., Rosa Parks, Harriet Tubman, and Nelson Mandela, are within some of the twenty-eight moments featured, but there is also a selection of athletes who paved the way to show that African American athletes can compete at the highest levels. Athletes such as Wilma Rudolph, Althea Gibson, Jesse Owens, Arthur Ashe, Jackie Robinson, and Hank Aaron are all celebrated in this text.

One of the common themes uniting the athletes throughout the book is their perseverance and athletic accomplishment amid adversity. Within the rhyming words of the poem, readers can learn about Jackie Robinson: "The first man of color to step up to a pro plate, rose through the ranks, despite taunts of hate" (Smith, 2015, pp. 23–24). They can also learn about how Hank Aaron, who received hate mail and death threats as he drew close to beating Babe Ruth's home run record because of his race, was encouraged by his fans' letters of support, which ultimately propelled him to achieve the baseball record.

Like the Eli Manning text in this section, teachers can use male athletic role models of the past to inspire male students and use them as a starting point to find other athletes who demonstrate athletic skill and strong character both inside and outside of the game.

Males with Physical Challenges

Physical differences are one of the reasons why a victim may be bullied. One of the ways to help overcome bullying is to learn about the ways others with physical differences have overcome adversity and accomplished their goals despite the odds. In this section, we discuss two nonfiction books that focus on the theme of males who have overcome physical challenges, which addresses Marilyn Price-Mitchell's (2015) defining qualities of a role model: someone who shows the ability to overcome obstacles.

The first recommended selection, *A Splash of Red: The Life and Art of Horace Pippin* (2013) by Jen Bryant, the 2014 Orbis Pictus Award winner, is a biography of the life of self-taught African American painter, Horace Pippin. With illustrations in Pippin's own style and his quotations colored throughout the book, the reader is immersed in the thoughts and images from the mind of this well-known artist.

Pippin was known for painting from his heart, often quoted saying, "Pictures just come to my mind . . . and I tell my heart to go ahead" (Bryant, 2013, p. 6). From the text, the reader can learn that Horace Pippin was not only known for his art, but he was also an honored member of the US military during World War I, which is where his physical challenges originated. An injured right arm from a bullet wound during battle earned Pippin a Purple Heart by the United States, but presented a significant challenge to his painting.

His injury caused a setback in finding a job upon return from the war and led to others doubting his physical and artistic abilities; however, the biography describes that during his life, even through poverty, racism, and injury, Pippin persevered. Despite his injury, Pippin discovered that with the use of a poker and using his strong arm as a guide for his injured arm, he could continue to pursue his passion, painting.

Although the bullying Pippin experienced is not explicitly stated in the text, the accompanying future reading and resources used by the author and illustrator in their research for this nonfiction book provide insights a teacher could share with students as additional research about the conditions Pippin overcame. Furthermore, young readers can look to Pippin's paintings themselves to learn more about the adversity Horace Pippin and his family faced, as slavery and segregation inspired many of his works.

Another inspiring true story of a boy with a physical challenge is told in *Emmanuel's Dream: The True Story of Emmanuel Ofosu Yeboah* (Thompson and Qualls, 2015). After Emmanuel was born with a deformed leg, his father abandoned the family, and many in the community thought he would become useless or a curse. However, as Emmanuel grew, he independently completed tasks that included fetching water for the family and hopping two miles to and from school. When no one would play with him, he saved money to buy a soccer ball to play with his friends, using crutches that his grandmother found. Eventually, Emmanuel gained the respect of his peers by playing soccer with one foot.

At the age of thirteen, Emmanuel traveled far to make money for his family; however, it took time for someone to hire him. Determined, Emmanuel found a food stand owner to hire him, and he continued to shine shoes to earn money for his family. After his mother passed away, he was heartbroken and determined to show the world that disability did not mean inability. The Challenged Athletes Foundation provided Emmanuel with equipment to ride a bike approximately four hundred miles across Ghana so that he could show others that having physical challenges did not equate to being cursed.

The authors share several instances of how Emmanuel reacted to bullies, including ignoring advice to beg instead of work and standing up to a shopkeeper who mistakenly scolded him for begging. Educators can emphasize these examples of how to cope with bullies and share Emmanuel's other successes mentioned in the author's note, such as his continued activism in helping others with physical challenges. Students might discuss what they could do to further help this cause, whether collaborating with some of Emmanuel's initiatives or creating their own.

A ROLE FOR BIOGRAPHIES IN THE CURRICULUM

Depending on the classroom and needs, educators can read one or more of these texts in a whole-class, small-group, or one-on-one setting. There are many ways in which these books can be used for bibliotherapy (McCulliss and Chamberlain, 2013; Wang, Couch, Rodriguez, and Lee, 2015), and we mention some in this section. If applicable, students should be encouraged to share their products, such as writing and art, with peers in a group to further facilitate discussion and learn from others (Senn, 2012).

1. Educators can embed salient questions when reading the text such as: How are you like any of the people in the book? Why would you want to be like one of these people? How would you like to change the story? What do you think will happen to one of these people in the next week or year?
2. Writing activities can be included before, during, or after the read-aloud. For example, students can write a poem, journal entry, or comic strip to express their feelings about being bullied. They could also write an opinion paper, write a letter to the role model, or write out possible solutions for the people bullied in the texts (especially for those that did not explicitly state how the role model coped).
3. Responding to text through art is another valuable activity. Students can sketch, paint, create an object or scene with clay, or make a collage from magazines to communicate their thoughts on bullying or positive role models featured in the texts.

4. The use of drama through role play, puppetry, and pantomime can also be therapeutic and empowering for students who have been bullied. For example, after reading *Emmanuel's Dream: The True Story of Emmanuel Ofosu Yeboah* (Thompson and Qualls, 2015), students can use Emmanuel's example of standing up to the store owner who thought he was a beggar to role-play a scenario of how they could articulate standing up for themselves and refrain from being bullied.

CONCLUDING REMARKS

What boys read has an impact on their character and personal values (Cypress and Anderson, 2011). As this chapter suggests, putting biographies of role models in boys' hands is an important step for educators and policymakers, as they can help boys find ways to cope with and/or prevent bullying, and promote social justice.

With the power of bibliotherapy and the practice of looking toward others who have been through similar social struggles, these book recommendations and ideas to integrate them into curricula just scratch the surface of how nonfiction can make a difference in tackling social issues and reducing inequity and oppression for all students, boys and girls alike.

We leave you with a call to action: Simply providing these books is not enough. Educators need to recommend these biographies with role models for students and choose books like these to read aloud in the classroom. The teacher's role is critical so students, especially boys, know that nonfiction is more than just for reading for information for academic purposes. They need to know that nonfiction can also provide emotional support for their personal lives. Booker T. Washington (1901) said that success is not measured as much by the position one reaches in life, but rather by the obstacles one has overcome. With these words in mind, let us show our boys examples of success in person, and through books.

REFERENCES

Allington, R. L., McGill-Franzen, A., Camilli, G., Williams, L., Graff, J., Zeig, J., Zmach, C., and Nowak, N. (2010). Ameliorating summer reading setback among economically disadvantaged elementary students. *Reading Psychology, 31*(5), 411–27.

Banks, J. A., Cookson, P., Gay, G., Hawley, W. D., Irvine, J. J., Nieto, S., Schofield, J. W., and Stephan, W. G. (2001). Diversity within unity: Essential principles for teaching and learning in a multicultural society. *Phi Delta Kappan, 83*(3), 196–98.

Barry, A. L. (2013). Reading preferences and perceptions of urban eighth graders. *Reading Horizons, 52*(4), 353–74.

Biskup, C., and Pfister, G. I would like to be like her/him: Are athletes role-models for boys and girls? *European Physical Education Review, 5*(3), 199–218.

Bricheno, P., and Thornton, M. (2007). Role model, hero or champion? Children's views concerning role models. *Educational Research, 49*(4), 383–96.

Brozo, W. (2006). Bridges to literacy for boys. *Educational Leadership, 64*(1), 71–74.
Cypress, A., and Lee-Anderson, K. (2011). The impact of boys and literacy: Connecting boys with books, engaging the adolescent reader. *International Journal of Interdisciplinary Social Sciences, 5*(10), 59–72.
De Vries, D., Brennan, Z., Lankin, M., Morse, R., Rix, B., and Beck, T. (2017). Healing with books. *Therapeutic Recreation Journal, 51*(1), 48–74.
Eisen, M. (2017). Eli Manning named co-winner of the Walter Payton Man of the Year Award. Retrieved from http://www.giants.com/news-and-blogs/article-1/Eli-Manning-named-co-winner-of-Walter-Payton-Man-of-the-Year-Award/e0e8b608-9b3f-4e7c-bd51-12a051fc0c2b.
Estrada, J., Garcia-Ael, C., and Martorell, J.L. (2015). Gender differences in adolescents' choices of heroes and admired adults in five countries. *Gender and Education, 27*(1), 69–87.
Gini, G., and Pozzoli, T. (2009). Association between bullying and psychosomatic problems: A meta-analysis. *Pediatrics, 123*(3), 1059–65.
Holub, S. C., Tisak, M. S., and Mullins, D. (2008). Gender differences in children's hero attributions: Personal hero choices and evaluations of typical male and female heroes. *Sex Roles, 58*(7–8), 567–78.
McCulliss, D. D., and Chamberlain, D. (2013). Bibliotherapy for youth and adolescents: School-based application and research. *Journal of Poetry Therapy, 26*(1), 13–40.
Nakamoto, J., and Schwartz, D. (2009). Is peer victimization associated with academic achievement? A meta-analytic review. *Social Development, 19*(2), 221–42.
National Center for Education Statistics. (2015). *The nation's report card.* Washington, DC: Institute of Education Sciences, US Department of Education.
Olweus, D. (1991). Bully/victim problems among schoolchildren. In D. J. Pepler and K. H. Rubin (Eds.), *The development and treatment of childhood aggression* (pp. 411–48). Hillsdale, NJ: Erlbaum.
Price-Mitchell, M. (2015). *Tomorrow's change makers: Reclaiming the power of citizenship for a new generation.* Bainbridge Island, WA: Eagle Harbor Publishing.
Senn, N. (2012). Effective approaches to motivate and engage reluctant boys in literacy. *The Reading Teacher, 66*(3), 211–20.
Sickmund, M., Sladky, T. J., Kang, W., and Puzzanchera, C. (2015). Easy access to the census of juveniles in residential placement. Retrieved from https://www.ojjdp.gov/ojstatbb/ezacjrp/.
Sourander, A., Jensen, P., Ronning, J.A., Niemela, S., Helenius, H., Sillanmaki, L., Kumpulainen, K., Piha, J., Tamminen, T., Moilanen, I., and Almqvist, F. (2007). What is the early adulthood outcome of boys who bully or are bullied in childhood? The Finnish "From a Boy to a Man" Study. *Pediatrics, 120*(2), 397–404.
US Department of Education. (2016). Student reports of bullying: Results from the 2015 school crime supplement to the National Crime Victimization Survey. Retrieved from https://nces.ed.gov/pubs2017/2017015.pdf.
Wang, C., Couch, L., Rodriguez, G., and Lee, C. (2015). The Bullying Literature Project: Using children's literature to promote prosocial behavior and social-emotional outcomes among elementary school students. *Contemporary School Psychology, 19*(4), 320–29.
Washington, B. T. (1901). *Up from slavery: An autobiography.* New York: Doubleday.
Williams, L. M. (2008). Book selections of economically disadvantaged Black elementary students. *Journal of Educational Research, 102*(1), 51–63.
Zambo, D. (2007). Using picture books to provide archetypes to young boys: Extending the ideas of William Brozo. *The Reading Teacher, 61*(2), 124–31.

CHILDREN'S BOOKS CITED

Bryant, J. (2013). *A splash of red: The life and art of Horace Pippin.* New York: Knopf Books.
Bunting, E. (1998). *Your move.* San Diego, CA: Harcourt Brace & Company.
Edwards, R. (2012). *Who is Barack Obama?* New York: Grosset & Dunlap.

MacRae, S. (2009). *Meet Eli Manning: Football's unstoppable quarterback*. New York: PowerKiDS Press.
Meltzer, B. (2010). *Heroes for my son.* New York: HarperCollins Publishers.
Meltzer, B. (2014). *I am Abraham Lincoln*. New York: Dial Group.
Smith, C. R. (2015). *28 days: Moments in Black history that changed the world*. New York: Roaring Book Press.
Thompson, L. A., and Qualls, S. (2015). *Emmanuel's dream: The true story of Emmanuel Ofosu Yeboah.* New York: Schwartz & Wade Books.

Chapter Eight

Creating Spaces for Critical Conversations on Issues of Social Justice

Mary Ellen Oslick, Terri Robertson, and Melissa Parks

This chapter examines an assignment in a new masters-level course for educating for social justice. Within the master's program, practicing teachers worked toward a degree focusing on advocating for socially marginalized students in local and global societies. This "theory to practice" degree program was founded upon the commitment to pedagogical practices that promote closing persistent and growing opportunity gaps (M.Ed. Elementary: Educating for Social Justice, 2015).

In the Content Area Literacy course, participants were asked to apply knowledge of critical literary theories in creating a book talk for an Orbis Pictus Award winner/honor book. While the book talks met the requirements of the assignment, the commentary for the critical perspectives of these nonfiction texts was disappointingly basic and shallow. Researchers discuss why practicing teachers seemed to struggle to read a nonfiction text with a critical lens and what scaffolding needs to be done for future teachers to be more successful in this endeavor.

Chapter 8
EXPLORING CRITICAL CONVERSATIONS IN NONFICTION TEXTS

The Space

In summer 2015, our university launched a "theory to practice" master's program for practicing teachers to enhance knowledge of teaching and ability to advocate for social change. The M.Ed. in Elementary Education program supports practicing teachers in developing innovative teaching methods and prepares them to enter leadership positions to *enact the system-wide changes in education that are needed to close the growing opportunity gap*. The Content Area Literacy course, in which this assignment was given, was taught toward the end of the program (after Critical Issues and Social Justice courses/experiences/readings) in the spring of 2016.

This course examines the use of multiple literacies for teaching and learning inside and outside of the classroom. Additionally, the course presents specific strategies designed to develop critical literacy skills that support learning across the curriculum and build on students' existing literacies. Specifically, one of the course objectives is to consider the complexity of literacy, critical literacy, and its potential for personal empowerment.

Teachers need to reflect on the benefits of using critical literacy strategies with their students. "Critical literacy can enhance comprehension, engagement, and interest for the students who are the most disenfranchised by literacy practices simply because these students are often already reading their world critically" (Rogers, 2014, p. 258). Using the strengths of all children within the classroom is an important tenet of social justice education.

Additionally, Lloyd and Wertsch (2016) argue that "nonfiction texts demand critical literacy" (p. 24). Using the five critical literacy practices described by Ciardiello (2004) can be a way for teachers to meet that demand. The critical literacy practices include examining multiple perspectives, finding an authentic voice, recognizing social barriers and overcoming borders of separation, regaining one's identity and listening and responding to "the call of service" (p. 138). The goal of these practices, as with any critical literacy curriculum, is to enable readers (e.g., students and teachers) to have critical conversations and become conscious consumers of texts.

The Conversation

Teachers enrolled in the course spent three class sessions (lasting three hours each) on the topics of critical literacy, critical literary theories, and finally, critical literary theory applications. First, scholarly articles defining critical literacy and sharing field examples were read (e.g., Aukerman, 2012; Labadie, Wetzel, and Rogers, 2012; Lewison, Flint, and Van Sluys, 2002). Students then reflected on their reading via a Questions/Issues/Connections response and shared their reflections in class. Next, critical literary theories were examined with familiar texts (e.g., *Little Red Riding Hood*).

In the final course session, participants were given a brief introduction to the National Council of Teachers of English Orbis Pictus Award, established in 1989 for promoting and recognizing excellence in the writing of nonfiction for children. The Orbis Pictus Award defines nonfiction as any title that has as its central purpose the sharing of information, including biography, but excluding textbooks, historical fiction, folklore, or poetry (http://www.ncte.org/awards/orbispictus).

As teachers are asked to incorporate greater variety of texts in their classrooms, the Orbis Pictus book list can be used to support both critical conversations of social justice and extend ideas from the text. The award committee selects nominations that should be useful in classroom teaching, should encourage thinking and more reading, model exemplary expository writing and research skills, share interesting and timely subject matter, and appeal to a wide range of ages.

Students were then asked to choose an award-winning or honor book to use with the following application assignment:

> You will be creating a book talk for an Orbis Pictus Award winner/honor book. After reading the book, you must apply a literary theory and find evidence to exemplify that perspective, and then present the significance of the book from that perspective. Use a technology of your choice (e.g., Prezi, VoiceThread, Glog, Popplet) to create a stylish and exciting book talk to hook readers (both students and other educators). In your book talk, please include the title of the book, author and illustrator names, one-sentence summary of the book, and at least three examples of evidence for the literary theory perspective of your choice.
>
> You will be graded on the following criteria:

- Overall product: all pieces of the book talk are included, quality is that of a masters-level course
- Evidence: choose the best evidence to support your point; evidence is highly persuasive and effective in supporting your argument
- Commentary: creative/original ideas and insights; extensive commentary, refreshing; goes beyond obvious and basic commentary
- Style: sophisticated vocabulary; evidence and commentary are smoothly blended
- Mechanics: no problems with coherence, grammar, spelling, or punctuation
- Technology: seamless use that enhances the book talk

The assignments (Prezis, VoiceThreads, and PowerPoints) were then examined.

WHAT WAS DISCOVERED?

Literary Theories Used

Most students participating in the study applied the Reader Response theory to the nonfiction text they chose to read. Rosenblatt's (1938/1995, 1978) transactional theory of reader response argues that what the reader brings to reading a text is just as important as what the author writes. When students and teachers read a text aesthetically, they bring with them specific social, political, and cultural factors that then influence their interactions with the story. These personal interpretations are both valid and desirable (Rosenblatt, 1978).

Additionally, Appleman (2009) states that readers are often most comfortable using this theory to critique texts. Five of ten graduate students who participated used this lens to analyze the Orbis Pictus text. Their responses connected to their own previous experiences and/or to the experiences of their students.

The second most-popular lens chosen to examine the texts was social class/Marxist theory. In a very basic way, this theory is grounded following the money and power embedded in a text. Some questions to guide thinking within this theory include: Who has the money/power? Who does not? What happens as a result? (Appleman, 2009). Three of ten graduate students who participated used this lens to analyze the text. Their analyses with the social class/Marxist lens went hand-in-hand with the content of the text (e.g., workers' rights, educational equality).

Finally, two graduate students who participated chose to use the lens of gender theory to examine their texts. This theory is similar to social class/Marxist theory, but instead of focusing on relationships between the classes, it focuses on relationships between the genders. Readers using this theory examine the patterns of thought, behavior, values, and power relations between the sexes (Appleman, 2009). The two texts used with this theory had young female protagonists.

Missed Opportunities

In this section, the work of three graduate students who participated (i.e., Graduate Student A, B, and C) is analyzed with specific examples of their critical literacy experiences in each of Lewison et al.'s (2002) four dimensions: disrupting the commonplace, interrogating multiple perspectives, focusing on sociopolitical issues, and promoting social justice. Some missed opportunities to engage in critical literacy practices and some possible future considerations are shared.

Graduate Student A

Graduate Student A chose *Parrots over Puerto Rico* (Roth and Trumbore, 2013) and used the Reader Response theory to relate the story to her own experiences growing up in Puerto Rico and the experiences of the English language learners she works with in a local elementary school. Her summary: "A picture book telling the intertwined histories of the Puerto Rican parrot and the island of Puerto Rico, culminating with current efforts to save the parrots from extinction."

She made some gains interacting in the critical literacy dimension of focusing on sociopolitical issues. "Being Puerto Rican is not just waiving [*sic*] our flag and putting it in our cars or participating in the miss universe contest. It is to know our history ... not as politicians tell it, but how it really happened." With this statement, she questioned the authors at several points in the story about their omission of details regarding the treatment of the indigenous people of Puerto Rico (Taino).

While the focus of the story is on how humans affected the parrots, Graduate Student A points out that foreigners (e.g., settlers from Spain and invaders from the United States) also affected Puerto Rico's native population.

Unfortunately, she stops her critique before she moves into the taking-action and promoting-social-justice dimension. With her recognition of the limitations in the book, she could have gone further to support a discussion with her students that did have resources addressing the treatment and decline of the indigenous people of Puerto Rico. A question to consider would be: Which people don't you hear in the story, and what might they say if you heard them? (Apol, 1998).

Her students could also create a Venn diagram to examine the major historical effects (e.g., Spanish settlers, slaves from Africa, and the Spanish-American War) on both the Puerto Ricans and the parrots. Finally, just as readers follow the current efforts of scientists in the Puerto Rican Parrot Recovery Program, they could research Taino heritage in modern times. What are contemporary Taino activists doing to preserve their culture?

Graduate Student B

Graduate Student B chose *Brave Girl: Clara and the Shirtwaist Makers' Strike of 1909* (Markel, 2013) and used the social class/Marxist lens to examine the text. Her summary:

> When Clara Lemlich arrived in America with her family, she couldn't speak English. Clara quickly learned that she would have to work and grow up fast to help her family make ends meet. Clara always had a positive attitude and spent

long hours learning English. She worked at a sewing factory in order to support her family. Clara quickly realized that something was not right.

Clara could not accept the fact that girls were being treated so unfairly. She wanted things to change and led the largest walkout of women workers in the country's history. She believed that everyone deserved a fair chance and if we stood together, we could make a big difference.

Graduate Student B made some attempts to engage in critical literacy with her text. After her summary slide, she gave an overview of the story with some important terms: immigrants, poor family, factory worker, hungry, injustice, and police brutality. These could be considered examples of her disrupting the commonplace, especially because of her background as a first-grade teacher.

By introducing these terms to her young students, she sets up some opportunities for difficult discussions. Although it was not explicitly stated, if she was to use this text in her classroom, Graduate Student B would be teaching her students to look at issues of class while inviting them to share their own personal connections with these terms as they read about Clara.

After the introduction of these terms, Graduate Student B included a PowerPoint slide that focused on the garment history between 1880 and 1920. This brings to light several important sociopolitical issues, such as the gender (female), age (between sixteen and twenty-five years old), and citizenship status (immigrants) of the workers. This context could be used to help readers examine the questions of who has money/power and who does not within the story.

These facts, however, are just listed at the end of the assignment. Graduate Student B fell short of considering ways to have students discuss such questions in the text. Furthermore, she could have gone beyond this one text and involved her students in an author-study approach to help them view writing as a powerful tool of personal expression (Fox, 2006). Markel is also the author of *Hillary Rodham Clinton: Some Girls Are Born to Lead* (2016). An author study would be a perfect time to ask students: What do you think the writer wants readers to think? (Appol, 1998).

Graduate Student C

Graduate Student C chose *Little Melba and Her Big Trombone* (Russell-Brown, 2014) and used the gender lens to examine the text. Her summary: "Brimming with exuberance and the joy of making music, *Little Melba and Her Big Trombone* is a lively tribute to a trailblazing musician and a great unsung hero of jazz."

She used basic assumptions from the gender lens to read the text and then justified these assumptions with evidence from the text. For example, she proposed the following author's purpose: "Given this perspective, the author is trying to say that it was very difficult during that time period for a woman to be a successful musician. Melba persevered through it all and let the music lead her life in the right direction." By doing this, Graduate Student C may have been engaged in the interrogating multiple viewpoints dimension of critical literacy.

One major missed opportunity was for her to examine sociopolitical issues within the text. Melba certainly struggled as a female musician, but Graduate Student C never mentions how the struggles were compounded with her race. How would Melba's experiences have been different if she were a white female? Drafting (or just considering) an interior monologue of Melba could have given Graduate Student C a deeper perspective (Bigelow and Christensen, 1994).

CRITICAL LITERACY AND SOCIAL JUSTICE: SOME CHALLENGES

So, why did this assignment flop? What impedes teachers' abilities and willingness to model and give time for critical literacy practices within their classrooms? Some teachers worry that there is one right way to practice critical literacy (Rogers, 2014), or they feel that their own educational experience was limited either concerning content or critical discourses (Riley and Crawford-Garrett, 2016).

Other teachers may be comfortable with more traditional privileges of discourse with right and wrong binaries usually favoring the teacher (Rogers, 2002). Including critical literacy practices in the classroom means that teachers must teach in an increasingly sophisticated manner (Rogers, 2014). This causes some teachers to worry about time for preparation and time for deep discussions within their classrooms.

Finally, teachers may worry about what parents, administrators, and/or other higher-ranking teachers will say, especially if the lens on which they frame the discussion is different from their own. Teachers who lack those experiences often hesitate to speak with authority. This contributes to either real or perceived peer pressure and can limit what materials and activities teachers feel they can use within their classrooms.

MOVING FORWARD

Placing critical literacy curriculum in the hands of teachers is the first step to enriching the educational experience for their students. Finding quality nonfiction literature can be a struggle, because the definition for nonfiction is nebulous. However, if you ask a teacher who has brought nonfiction books into the classroom where to start, they may tell you that the first tool needed is a desire and passion for bringing critical literature books into the classroom.

Along with this passion, the teacher needs to be willing to change current teaching practices to allow a space for critical literacy. As one of the teachers (Graduate Student in the study) in the course noted:

> I would have loved to have collaborated with a colleague on my book talk to enrich my lesson. Although I am at a school with many talented people, I have discovered that many of my colleagues are unaware of critical literacy use in the classroom. Even if time was plentiful, discussions would require background on the topic before meaningful discussions could occur.

For many teachers, support is needed to depart from current practices and embrace nonfiction in the classroom. Teachers work in an age when scripted curriculum maps and modules are mandated by their districts. However, this curriculum doesn't need to be disregarded. Instead, teachers can use and tailor the current curriculum while embedding elements of critical literacy simultaneously.

Along with twenty-first-century skills gaining importance with the new standards, nonfiction is also becoming the new staple in most classrooms. Teachers can use this to their advantage because embedding critical literacy into curriculum is actually embracing the new standards.

Asking teachers to take time to embed critical literacy lessons into their plans means that they need to be given the time to plan and the support system to do so. Subsequently, colleagues who are like-minded regarding the importance of enriching the classroom with nonfiction should be allowed to meet and plan together. Having support from other teachers who are diving into critical literature along with you makes a big difference in teacher attitudes and experiences.

Embracing nonfiction in your classroom can also be very dependent upon the support of your principal. Approaching your principal with your standards-based plan of action and your desired results would be one way to gain support. Another way is to create your own planned learning community through the Internet, such as accessing other teachers through Twitter. Ask your principal if you can facilitate curriculum planning meetings interconnected to critical literacy.

Research shows that teachers who use a wide variety of literacy materials and integrate content into all areas of instruction are effective teachers (Allington, Johnston, and Day, 2002; Presley et al., 2001). During these meetings, take a common theme and find ways to weave it into the standard curriculum, using the literature piece as the focus and the standards as the framework.

The following critical literacy strategies have been compiled from scholarly works and could be used in conjunction with nonfiction texts.

1. Have students write an interior monologue of a main character that can foster empathy (Bigelow and Christensen, 1994).
2. Involve students in an author-study approach to help them view writing as a powerful tool of personal expression (Fox, 2006).
3. Questions to be used with young children (Apol, 1998):

- *How are characters and situations portrayed?*
    - Who do you like in the story?
    - Who is always in the background in this story?
    - Which people don't you hear in the story, and what might they say if you heard them?

- *How is information presented?*
    - Are there other ways to show this person/place/event?

- *How is the text intended to be read?*
    - What do you think the writer wants readers to think?

- *How do they as readers respond to the text?*
    - What did you notice about this story?
    - How does this make you feel?

This research study used the Orbis Pictus Award winners and honors, but this award is not without its own critiques. Crisp (2015) analyzed past nominees and shared his concerns that the books nominated had the following issues: notable gender bias favoring males; most focal subjects were dead (when submitted); and region, religion, and socioeconomic status were single-focused on white, American middle-class males.

These concerns were valid at the time; however, the recent Orbis Pictus nominees (2016–2017) are varied in focal subjects. Not only do a majority of the books nominated represent diversity, but it seems to be the focus. The Orbis Pictus committee may have been mindful of Crisp's criticism when nominating outstanding pieces of literature or there may have been a small shift in publishing more diverse books for the committee to review.

FINAL THOUGHTS

"There's gold in every mistake" (Frasier, 2009). This quote from a familiar children's book appropriately sums up this project. While the assignment did not go as planned for the course within a master's program focused on social justice, the researchers and graduate students learned some valuable lessons. As mentioned previously, teachers worry about practicing critical literacy the right way, with the right information, and they may not even have experience with critical discourses (Riley and Crawford-Garrett, 2016; Rogers, 2002, 2014).

This research serves as evidence that resources and professional development is needed in elementary schools to support teacher growth with critical literacy practices. Future projects may include teacher book clubs that give both time and the chance to examine quality nonfiction literature with a critical lens before sharing the text with students. As teachers increase their understanding and practice with critical conversations in their classrooms, beginning a lesson study with trusted colleagues would be the natural progression for improving practice and students' learning experiences.

REFERENCES

Allington, R., Johnston, P., and Day, J. P. (2002). Exemplary fourth-grade teachers. *Language Arts, 79*(6), 462–66.
Apol, L. (1998). "But what does this have to do with kids?" Literary theory in children's literature in the children's literature classroom. *Journal of Children's Literature, 24*(2), 32–46.
Appleman, D. (2009). *Critical encounters in high school English.* New York: Teachers College Press.
Bigelow, B., and Christensen, L. (1994). Promoting social imagination through interior monologues. In B. Bigelow (Ed.), *Rethinking our classrooms: Teaching for equity and justice* (pp. 110–11). Milwaukee: Rethinking Schools.
Ciardiello, A. V. (2004). Democracy's young heroes: An instructional model of critical literacy practices. *The Reading Teacher, 58*(2), 138–47.
Crisp, T. (2015). A content analysis of Orbis Pictus award-winning nonfiction, 1990–2014. *Language Arts, 92*(4), 241–55.
Fox, K. R. (2006, November/December). Using author studies in children's literature to explore social justice issues. *The Social Studies,* 251–56.
Lewison, M., Flint, A. S., and Van Sluys, K. (2002). Taking on critical literacy: The journey of newcomers and novices. *Language Arts, 79*(5), 382–92.
Lloyd, R. M., and Wertsch, S. (2016). "Why doesn't anyone know this story?": Integrating critical literacy and informational reading. *English Journal, 105*(4), 24–30.
Pressley, M., Wharton-McDonald, R., Allington, R., Block, C. C., Morrow, L., Tracy, D., Baker, K., Brooks, G., Cronin, J., Nelson, E., and Woo, D. (2001). A study of effective first-grade literacy instruction. *Scientific Studies of Reading, 5*(1), 35–58.
Riley, K. and Crawford-Garrett, K. (2016). Critical text in literacy teacher education: Living inquiries into racial justice and immigration. *Language Arts, 94*(2), 94–107.
Rogers, R. (2002). "That's what you're here for, you're supposed to tell us": Teaching and learning critical literacy. *Journal of Adolescent and Adult Literacy, 45*(8), 772–87.

Rogers, R. (2014). Coaching literacy teachers as they design critical literacy practices. *Reading and Writing Quarterly, 30*(3), 241–61.
Rosenblatt, L. M. (1978). *The reader, the text, the poem.* Carbondale, IL: Southern Illinois University.
Rosenblatt, L. M. (1938/1995). *Literature as exploration.* New York: MLA.

CHILDREN'S BOOKS CITED

Frasier, D. (2009). *Miss Alaineus: A vocabulary disaster.* Boston: HMH Books for Young Readers.
Markel, M. (2013). *Brave girl: Clara and the shirtwaist makers' strike of 1909.* New York: Balzer + Bray.
Markel, M. (2016). *Hillary Rodham Clinton: Some girls are born to lead.* New York: HarperCollins Publishers.
Roth, S. L., and Trumbore, C. (2013). *Parrots over Puerto Rico.* New York: Lee & Low Books.
Russell-Brown, K. (2014). *Little Melba and her big trombone.* New York: Lee & Low Books.
Tonatiuh, D. (2014). *Separate is never equal.* New York: Abrams Books.

Chapter Nine

Helpful Resources to Engage Children in Conversations on Social Issues in Nonfiction Literature

Suzanne Chapman, Mario Worlds, and Soowon Jo

As the world continues to struggle with issues of racial, gender, sexual, and disability inequalities, both in and out of school, many educators turn to literature as a tool for promoting dialogue about these challenging topics. Literature helps students make sense of the many inequities that occur and reaffirm the need for social justice work. Through literature, students not only read words or texts, but also learn to "read the world" (Freire & Macedo, 1987). The reading of the world helps them understand social issues that continually impact marginalized groups of people and empowers them to become involved in conversations and community actions that seek to fight for social justice.

These conversations that can happen as a result of exposure to texts that focus on social justice are a key element in "problem-posing education" (Freire, 1970). As students engage with the literature, teachers are encouraged to be participants in authentic dialogue that helps all classroom members consider their existence in the world and their potential roles in transforming it for the betterment of humanity. As Gallo (1994) stated, "If we do not provide our students with a variety of literature—however controversial—and teach them to read it and discuss it critically, we cannot hope that they will ever develop into sensitive, thoughtful, and reasonable adults" (p. 118).

For teachers wanting to transform their classrooms into critical spaces where important dialogue about social justice issues take place, there are a number of resources available to help them begin much-needed dialogue with their students. In this chapter, we present resources available for identifying nonfiction literature that can be used to promote conversations on social issues with students. These resources include book awards, texts, and websites that focus on instruction with books of diversity. In the following sections, these resources are described.

AWARDS AND RECOGNITION FOR CHILDREN'S AND YOUNG ADULT NONFICTION LITERATURE

In the recent past, books of nonfiction were an underappreciated genre of literature for children and young adults (Kiefer, 2010). From the early 1920s to the early 1980s, only six nonfiction books won the Newbery Medal. During the same time period, nonfiction works were often dominating the lists of bestsellers in adult literature (Bacon, 1981). In 1990, the National Council of Teachers of English established the Orbis Pictus Award for Outstanding Nonfiction for Children to alleviate this disparity.

Thereafter, many awards in children's and young adult literature were established. These award-winning book lists serve as a helpful reference for teachers when engaging students in conversations on social issues. All of the books included on the lists have been examined by experts and scholars for aspects of accuracy of presented information, appropriateness for intended readers, format, and quality of content.

A few of the established awards are specifically intended to honor nonfiction or informational books of excellence, whereas others are given to the books and authors that promote the awareness of social issues including topics of social justice, equality, and peace. The following list includes a description of these awards and their respective websites.

Orbis Pictus Award for Outstanding Nonfiction for Children: Sponsored by the committee of the National Council of Teachers of English, this award recognizes nonfiction books that have been published in the United States for their excellence in writing (http://www.ncte.org/awards/orbispictus).

Robert F. Sibert Information Book Medal: Established by the Association for Library Service to Children, this annual award is given to the author(s) and illustrator(s) of the most outstanding informational book published in the English language in the preceding year (http://www.ala.org/alsc/awardsgrants/bookmedia/sibertmedal).

Jane Addams Children's Book Award: This award is presented annually to the children's books published in the preceding year that most effectively promote children's thinking and discussion of peace, equality, dignity, social justice, and world community with literary merit (http://www.janeaddamspeace.org/jacba/).

Notable Books for a Global Society: As part of the International Literacy Association, the committee of Children's Literature and Reading Special Interest Group selects twenty-five trade books of excellence for promoting readers' understandings of people and cultures throughout the world. Books for kindergarten through twelfth-grade students in all genres are reviewed for this award (http://www.clrsig.org/nbgs.php).

YALSA Award for Excellence in Nonfiction for Young Adults: By the Young Adult Library Services Association of the American Library Association, the YALSA Award for Excellence in Nonfiction is presented to the best nonfiction book published during a November 1 to October 31 publishing year for young adults, ages twelve to eighteen (http://www.ala.org/yalsa/nonfiction).

Carter G. Woodson Book Award: Every year, the National Council for Social Studies grants the Carter G. Woodson Book Awards to the most outstanding social studies books. The books are primarily nonfiction texts that sensitively and accurately depict topics related to ethnic minorities in the United States (https://www.socialstudies.org/awards/woodson/winners).

Washington Post Children's Books Guide Nonfiction Award: This award is given to an author or illustrator for a body of work in juvenile informational books (https://childrensbookguild.org/).

AWARD-WINNING NONFICTION FOCUSING ON SOCIAL ISSUES

An excellent starting point for engaging children, specifically secondary students, in conversations on social issues in nonfiction literature are texts that reflect social movements. Learning about social movements provides students with opportunities to witness the agency and courage individuals exhibit when struggling to bring about social change (Kelly, Minnes Brandes, & Orlowski, 2004). *March: Book One* (2013), the first book of a graphic novel trilogy that explores the life of John Lewis, is an excellent nonfiction choice to help students begin having conversations about social justice issues, specifically those related to civil rights. This graphic novel chronicles the life of Congressman John Lewis and his fight for equality and freedom.

A prominent figure during the civil rights movement, Congressman Lewis shares his experience as a young civil rights activist struggling to bring about change during a time when racism and segregation defined the United States, particularly in the South. The first book in this trilogy explores the congressman's formative years within the movement and looks at the ways in which his childhood experiences growing up in rural Alabama would later shape much of the work for which he became known.

From meeting Dr. Martin Luther King Jr. to his involvement in Nashville Student Movement and nonviolent protests like sit-ins, Congressman Lewis exhibited a tremendous amount of courage, even at a young age. *March* is a thought-provoking novel that students and teachers can undoubtedly learn from. A recipient of many awards (e.g., American Library Association Notable Book and Coretta Scott King Honor Book), this graphic novel not only provides a small historical lesson about the civil rights movement, it also provides a reference point from which students are able to understand and contextualize existing social movements today.

Among the many social movements that have begun to reemerge are movements supporting women's rights and gender equality. As women have continued a longstanding tradition of political and social engagement, the number of arenas through which women express their voice and concerns for equals rights have also increased. Literature has continued to represent a means of disseminating social commentary and necessary critiques about social issues that women face.

Given that school is frequently a site of gender discrimination (Ara & Malik, 2012), it makes sense, then, that secondary teachers engage their students in conversations about gender rights and the treatment of women. Arguably the most visible face related to recent women's movements/marches has been Hillary Clinton. A biography, *Hillary Clinton: A Woman Living History*, written by Karen Blumenthal, speaks to many issues concerning women's rights. A YALSA 2017 finalist for nonfiction, this biography details the early life of Hillary Clinton and her many achievements.

Despite an overwhelming number of accomplishments in public service, including serving as an attorney, senator, US secretary of state, first lady, and her historic run for president, she faced unparalleled criticism. While her gender rendered her susceptible to intense scrutiny, this work shares her unwavering commitment to public service, even in the face of many obstacles.

Like books previously mentioned, nonfiction literature that focuses on social justice issues often speak to individuals or groups who trail blaze paths for other marginalized people. The same can be said for members of the LGBTQ community, who have been inspired and encouraged by other brave members of the LGBTQ who courageously share their experiences. For teachers working with students, those who do and do not identify as LGBTQ, it is increasingly imperative to share narratives centered around the struggle for LGBTQ rights.

Ivan Coyote's (2016) *Tomboy Survival Guide* is a wonderful text to help students begin to understand gender identity and respect the experiences of men and women who identify in various ways. A 2017 Stonewall Book Award–Israel Fishman Nonfiction honor book, this book shares the story of a "tomboy" and their ability to understand themselves and help others come to terms with their own sexual and gender identities. Coyote, who identifies using the pronoun "they," shares their story, not just of coming of age, but also coming to terms with who they were and their true identity.

The humorous memoir explores the many ways in which gender binaries are oppressive to those who refuse to conform to such rigid definitions of identity. By sharing their own experiences, Coyote essentially provides a "guide" or a path for others who may struggle navigating gender, sexuality, and identity while empowering others to create a path of their own.

Nonfiction literature that addresses issues of social justice provides insight into the experiences of people who are often marginalized. Literature offers a place for their stories to be heard and represented in ways that are generally not celebrated within the larger society. Like African Americans, women, and members of the LGBTQ community, Asian Americans have a rich history that entails issues of social justice that is too often ignored.

Martin Sandler's (2013) work, *Imprisoned: The Betrayal of Japanese Americans During WWII*, challenges young readers to reconsider what it means to be free in a nation that is supposed to be founded on freedom and equality for all.

This riveting novel gives an account of Pearl Harbor and the war's impact on Japanese Americans living within the country. Relying on interviews and oral stories told by Japanese Americans who survived the brutality of internment camps, Sandler (2013) provides a unique and rare insight into the prejudice and discrimination that larger numbers of citizens were subjected to here in America.

A 2013 winner of YALSA Awards for Excellence in Nonfiction, *Imprisoned: The Betrayal of Japanese Americans During WWII* offers a critique of what it means to serve one's country while simultaneously being enslaved and subjected to discrimination. This novel helps young readers explore the dangers of racism, prejudice, and the hysteria that stems from fear of certain racial, cultural, and ethnic groups.

MULTIMEDIA RESOURCES

In addition to the aforementioned book awards and award-winning texts, teachers also have access to an abundance of online resources that are intended to help promote critical conversations on issues of social justice. Some of the resources are Internet pages that can be located through a quick online search. Other resources can be located through the use of popular social media outlets like Facebook, Pinterest, or Twitter. In the following section, a handful of these resources are described.

We Need Diverse Books: This website is designated to promoting access to books of diversity for all students. In their definition of *diversity*, the site indicates that they include (but do not limit their definition to) "LGBTQIA, Native, people of color, gender diversity, people with disabilities, and ethnic, cultural, and religious minorities" (http://weneeddiversebooks.org/mission-statement/). Within this website, educators can find a link to a resources page titled, "Where to Find Diverse Books."

This page contains a plethora of linked resources for educators seeking lists of books on diversity. Although all of the texts listed are not nonfiction resources, there is an abundance that do fit within this category. The resources on the page are sorted by topic (e.g., African American, American Indian, Disabilities, LGBTQIA). The list also provides links to a large number of the previously mentioned book awards focusing on diversity and includes additional awards (e.g., Coretta Scott King Book Awards, The Stonewall Book Awards, The Arab American Book Award). http://weneeddiversebooks.org/.

Cult of Pedagogy: A Collection of Resources for Teaching Social Justice: This website serves as an informational hub for identifying a number of resources for teaching social justice in the classroom. Embedded links within the webpage can lead teachers to podcasts, blogs, lesson plans, videos, and academic articles that focus issues of social justice. The author provides helpful hints and guidelines for those new to teaching with more controversial texts, as books of social justice can often be.

Many of these resources (e.g., audio files) can be used to more deeply explore topics discussed from nonfiction texts. For example, within the website, the viewer could click on a link that directs them to a page created by the Gay, Lesbian, and Straight Education Network (GLESN) (https://www.glsen.org/unheardvoices.html). This link will lead them to transcripts and recorded interviews of those who helped shape the history of the LGBT movement.

This site provides a multitude of links to many other websites focusing on social justice education. Be sure to also look in the "viewer comments" section, as many who subscribe to the site also share some of their favorite online resources (https://www.cultofpedagogy.com/social-justice-resources/).

Social Justice Books: A Teaching for Change Project: This website provides students and educators with an abundance of textual resources for examining topics of multiculturalism and social justice. Although the site includes a mix of narrative and nonfiction titles, the site contains over fifty booklists that do include nonfiction (e.g., Africa, Asian American, economic class, different abilities, holidays). By clicking on any of the booklist links, the viewer is directed to a page of texts that have been sorted by audience (e.g., elementary, middle, young adult).

Each text title also links the viewer to a synopsis of the book and reviews. Additionally, each booklist contains instructional texts and articles intended for teachers to use as they explore each of the topics with their students. Finally, the site provides teachers with a guide for evaluating and selecting anti-bias children's books (https://socialjusticebooks.org/).

Locating Resources on Facebook: Social media provides a number of resources that can help teachers remain updated on current trends and topics in the area of children's literature. By "liking" or subscribing to Facebook pages of different literary organizations, teachers gain access to booklists, articles, and resources for teaching a multitude of topics in their classroom. Teachers may consider subscribing to pages created by The Horn Book, The Center for the Study of Multicultural Children's Literature, American Libraries Magazine, or Children's Literature Assembly.

These Facebook pages are continually uploading new content that can greatly help subscribers as they search for resources on any topic, including social issues. For example, American Libraries Magazine recently posted links to informative pieces published by YALSA regarding narrative nonfiction with social justice themes (http://www.yalsa.ala.org/thehub/2016/12/06/narrative-nonfiction-social-justice/) and evaluating materials containing characters with disabilities (http://www.yalsa.ala.org/thehub/2016/12/18/social-justice-disability-evaluating-materials-media-characters-disabilities/).

Locating Resources on Twitter: Other multimedia platforms such as Twitter also provide quick access to nonfiction writing that teachers and students can use to facilitate discussions on current social justice issues. For example, "hashtag advocacy" is the use of technology such as Twitter hashtags to learn more about and participate in social justice movements.

Many of the current movements focusing on social issues, such as Black Lives Matter (#BLM), Bring Back Our Girls (#BringBackOurGirls), Dakota access pipeline (#NoDAPL and #StandingWithStandingRock), and climate change (#ClimateChange), began with the use of hashtags on the social network Twitter.

By simply searching a particular hashtag, teachers and students are not only able to view and participate in national and global discussions about certain social justice movements, they gain access to nonfiction or informational writing like news reports, articles, blogs, and written accounts of social justice issues that are nonfiction. By incorporating multimedia in classroom discussions about social justice, teachers not only offer a new source for locating nonfiction texts but also force students to reconsider what is defined as nonfiction literature.

Locating Resources on Pinterest: A final social network that provides helpful resources for teachers researching materials for social justice education is Pinterest. On this multimedia tool, teachers can simply type in a keyword search of "social justice education" and they are provided a list of "pins" they can sort through and save to their own boards for future reference. An example of a site that can be "pinned" is provided by an organization called *Doing Good Together*.

In this particular resource, readers are provided a list of fiction and nonfiction books that can be used for promoting equality. Like previously mentioned websites, the page provides a list of books organized by category (e.g., Civil Rights Movement, Disability Rights Movement) and also includes conversation starters for teachers and parents to use as they talk about the books with children (http://www.doinggoodtogether.org/bhf-book-lists/chapter-books-to-fuel-social-justice).

Instructional Resources for Specific Titles: When a teacher finds a specific book they have identified as a useful resource to support dialogue about social issues, it may also be worth their time to search the Internet for a specific website designated to that particular title. For example, a recent notable piece of nonfiction titled *I Dissent: Ruth Bader Ginsburg Makes Her Mark* (Levy & Baddeley, 2016) is a picture book biography of the popular Supreme Court justice and her continued fight for equal rights among many marginalized groups.

The book has won more than twelve awards and has garnered rave reviews. The book's author, Debbie Levy, has a website providing instructional resources for a number of her children's books. Included in the resources on this book's page are multiple curriculum guides for tips on instructing with the book, a link to Ruth Bader Ginsburg's blog, and interviews with Ruth Bader Ginsburg herself. The site is certainly a useful tool for any teacher including this text for instruction (http://debbielevybooks.com/books/i-dissent-ruth-bader-ginsburg-makes-her-mark/?tn=0).

INCORPORATING THESE RESOURCES INTO THE CURRICULA

When it comes to presenting literature on social issues, teachers may have a tendency to shy away from texts that feel too challenging or controversial. Rather, they choose to stay in a safe zone where all the books presented have a happy ending. However, real-life issues do not always end happily. In fact, real life is full of challenging issues that leave us with questions for which we do not have immediate answers. Yet it is within this place of problem-posing and dialogue that real learning can take place (Freire, 1970). This was found to be the case in four classrooms described in an article by Lewison and Leland (2002).

In their work, the authors explored the use of historic and realistic fiction as a tool for exploring diversity and democracy. The four participating classrooms varied in developmental ranges from kindergarten to college level. However, in all cases, the authors found that literature was a powerful tool in inviting students to engage in conversations about difficult social issues.

Rather than shelter children from these challenging topics, Lewison and Leland (2002) suggest that we provide students a safe space for inquiry where they can use the literature presented as a springboard for having meaningful conversations about these challenging topics. All of the resources presented in this chapter provide teachers with an abundance of instructional tools for having important and necessary conversations with students about current and sometimes controversial topics of social issues. Although some of the topics may feel a bit risky for teachers as they first embark on this journey, we must develop a space for children to communicate about these topics if we expect them to grow into compassionate, empathic, and socially responsible adults.

REFERENCES

Ara, N., and Malik, S. K. (2012). Gender discrimination in education: A barrier in development of female education at higher secondary level. *Interdisciplinary Journal of Contemporary Research in Business, 4*(5), 330–39.

Bacon, B. (1981). The art of nonfiction. *Children's Literature in Education, 12*(1), 3–14.

Freire, P. (1970). *Pedagogy of the oppressed.* New York, NY: Continuum International.

Freire, P., and Macedo, D. P. (1987). *Literacy: reading the word & the world.* South Hadley, MA: Bergin & Garvey Publishers.

Gallo, D. R. (1994). Censorship of young adult literature. In J. S. Simmons (ed.), *Censorship, a threat to reading, learning and thinking* (pp. 115–22). Newark, DE: International Reading Association.

Kelly, D. M., Minnes Brandes, G., and Orlowski, P. (2004). Teaching for social justice: Veteran high school teachers' perspectives. *Scholarly Practitioner Quarterly, 2*(2), 39–57.

Kiefer, B. Z. (2010). *Charlotte Huck's children's literature* (tenth edition). New York, NY: McGrawHill.

Lewison, M., and Leland, C. (2002). Dangerous discourses: using controversial books to support engagement, diversity, and democracy. *The New Advocate, 15*(3), 215–26.

CHILDREN'S LITERATURE CITED

Blumenthal, K. (2016). *Hillary Rodham Clinton: A woman living history.* New York, NY: Feiwel and Friends.

Coyote, I. (2016). *Tomboy survival guide.* Vancouver, Canada: Arsenal Pulp Press.

Levy, D., and Baddeley, E. (2016). *I dissent: Ruth Bader Ginsburg makes her mark.* New York, NY: Simon & Schuster.

Lewis, J., Aydin, A., and Powell, N. (2013). *March.* Marietta, GA: Top Shelf Productions.

Sandler, M. W. (2013). *Imprisoned: The betrayal of Japanese Americans during WWII*. New York: Bloomsbury.

Appendix A

A Framework for a Curriculum That Is International

A Framework for a Curriculum That Is International (Short, 2009, p.3).

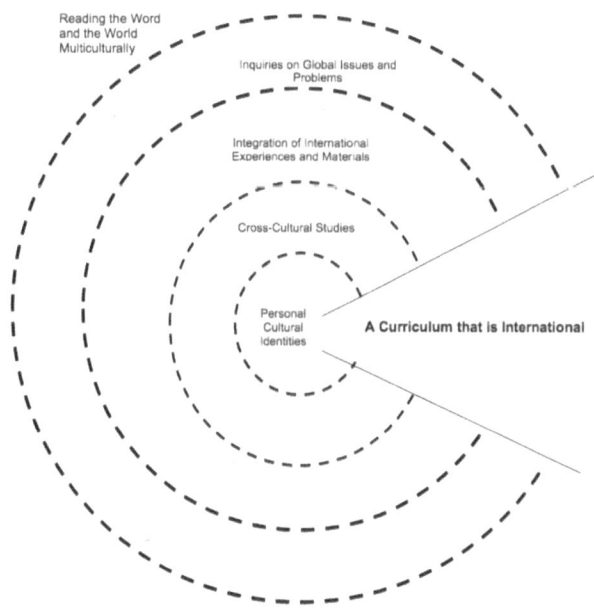

A Frame Work for Curriculum That Is International. *Bookbird: A Journal of International Children's Literature*, 47(2): 1–10.

Appendix B

Know, Want to Know, Learned Chart Example

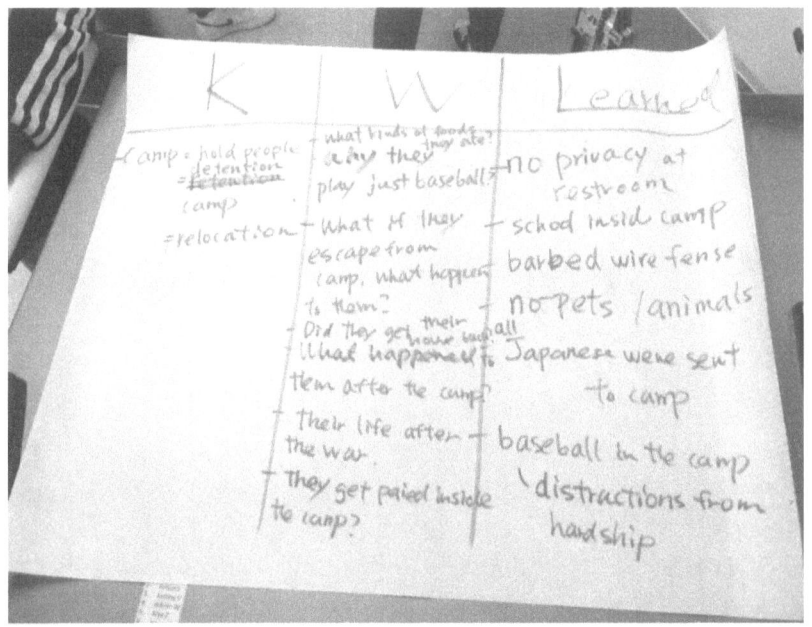

KWL Chart example.

Appendix C

Graffiti Board Example

Graffiti Board example: Students wrote/sketched their connections, surprises, and questions while reading nonfiction and fiction texts. The sixth grade class.

Appendix D

Graffiti Board Example

Students are writing and sketching their responses on Graffiti Board while reading *A Diamond in the Desert*. The sixth grade class.

About the Editors

Vivian Yenika-Agbaw is professor of children's literature in the Department of Curriculum and Instruction at The Pennsylvania State University, University Park, where she teaches undergraduate and graduate courses in children's/adolescent literature. She has published numerous articles and authored/coedited several books, including *Adolescents Rewrite their Worlds: Using Literature to Illustrate Writing Forms* (Rowman & Littlefield, 2015); *African Youth in Contemporary Literature and Popular Culture: Identity Quest* (2014); and *Fairy Tales with a Black Consciousness: Essays on Adaptations of Familiar Stories* (2013). She has taught children's literature in the Departments of Curriculum and Instruction and English at state universities in Pennsylvania (Clarion and Bloomsburg), and has taught high school English abroad and in the United States. Yenika-Agbaw has served on several editorial boards and reviewed manuscripts for *Children's Literature in Education*, *Children's Literature*, and the *Journal of Children's Literature*. She is currently serving on the International Research Society for Children's Literature Board (2017–2019). Yenika-Agbaw is also an active member of the National Council of Teachers of English (NCTE) and Children's Literature Association (ChLA).

Ruth McKoy Lowery is professor of literacy and associate chair of the Department of Teaching and Learning at The Ohio State University. She teaches courses on children's literature and literacy education. Her current research focuses on children's literature—particularly immigrant and multicultural literature, the adaptation of immigrant and at-risk students in schools, and preparing teachers to teach a diverse student population. Lowery is an active member of the National Council of Teachers of English, the

International Literacy Association, and the US Board on Books for Young People.

Paul H. Ricks is a doctoral candidate in curriculum and instruction at The Pennsylvania State University, where he currently teaches children's literature courses. Last year, he was a visiting instructor of children's literature at Brigham Young University, and prior to that he also taught fifth and sixth grade in Salt Lake City, Utah, for seven years. Through international teaching experiences in Mozambique and Brazil, Ricks developed interests in cross-cultural studies and translations of Spanish and Portuguese texts. His articles have appeared in *The Dragon Lode*, *Literacy Research and Instruction*, *The Reading Teacher*, and *Literacy Today*.

About the Contributors

Ann Berger-Knorr, PhD, is an associate professor of education at Lebanon Valley College. She is also the Alpha Zeta Tau chapter counselor of Kappa Delta Pi, International Honor Society in Education. She is a contributing column author in *Pennsylvania Reads, Journal of The Keystone State Reading Association*. She also currently serves on the manuscript review board for *The Dragon Lode*. Berger-Knorr teaches courses in literacy, literature, and research methods. In her research, Berger-Knorr attempts to bridge teacher education, literacy education, and multicultural education. Utilizing teacher research and classroom inquiry, Berger-Knorr focuses on ways to best prepare preservice teachers for culturally and academically diverse kindergarten through eighth-grade settings.

Suzanne C. Chapman, PhD, is a lecturer in the School of Teaching and Learning at the University of Florida. She earned her MEd and EdS in curriculum and instruction from the University of Florida in 2000 and 2005, respectively. Chapman has eight years of experience in Title 1 education, working as a first-grade teacher, as a secondary-level intensive reading teacher, and as a reading coach. In 2015, she completed her PhD at the University of Florida in curriculum and instruction, concentrating on literacy and language education. Her research interests include topics in disciplinary literacy and children's literature. Chapman can be contacted at schapman@coe.ufl.edu.

Kathleen Colantonio-Yurko is currently an assistant professor of literacy at the State University of New York, Brockport. Before she became a professor, Colantonio-Yurko worked as a middle and high school teacher in Florida for nine years. In her current role, she works with preservice teachers and instructs multiple literacy courses. Colantonio-Yurko earned her doctorate in curriculum and instruction with specialties in English language arts education, literacy, and children's literature. Her dissertation focused on the low performance of otherwise capable students in their secondary English language arts courses. Much of her current research explores the use of multicultural texts and young adult literature in the secondary English language arts classroom and how these texts can be used to understand social justice issues.

Deanna Day teaches undergraduate and graduate literacy and technology courses for Washington State University. She has served on the Notable Children's Books in the Language Arts Award and the Notable Books for Global Society committees. She also reviews children's literature for *The Dragon Lode*.

Soowon Jo is a doctoral candidate in the College of Education at the University of Florida. Specializing in children's literature, her research interests include literacy learning through children's literature and writing, and teacher education. She has taught Children's Literature and Language Arts methods courses for elementary and early childhood teacher preparation programs. Jo can be contacted at soowonjo@ufl.edu.

Ruth McKoy Lowery is professor of literacy and associate chair of the Department of Teaching and Learning at The Ohio State University. She teaches courses on children's literature and literacy education. Her current research focuses on children's literature—particularly immigrant and multicultural literature, the adaptation of immigrant and at-risk students in schools, and preparing teachers to teach a diverse student population. Lowery is an active member of the National Council of Teachers of English, the International Literacy Association, and the US Board on Books for Young People.

Cody Miller teaches ninth-grade English language arts at P.K. Yonge Developmental Research School, the University of Florida's affiliated K12 laboratory school. In addition to teaching, Miller is currently a PhD student in English education at the University of Florida.

Mary Napoli, PhD, is an associate professor of reading and children's literature at Penn State Harrisburg where she teaches undergraduate and graduate courses in literacy, literature, and literacy leadership. Napoli's research has been published in the *Journal of Children's Literature*, *Kappa Delta Pi Record*, *Childhood Education*, and *The Journal of Reading, Writing, and Literacy*. She is the coauthor or editor of five books and is the author or coauthor of numerous book chapters. Currently, Napoli serves as the children's literature section review editor of *The Dragon Lode*. Her current research interests include how teachers infuse critical literacy and diverse literature across the curriculum.

Mary Ellen Oslick is an assistant professor of literacy/reading at Stetson University in DeLand, Florida. Her research areas of interest include social justice and critical literacy applications; multicultural children's literature; and reading and writing instruction with diverse learners.

Melissa Parks is an assistant professor of teacher education at Stetson University in DeLand, Florida. Her research areas of interests include elementary pedagogies; science, technology, engineering, and mathematics education; and preservice teacher efficacy.

Paul H. Ricks is a doctoral candidate in curriculum and instruction at The Pennsylvania State University where he currently teaches children's literature courses. Last year, he was a visiting instructor of children's literature at Brigham Young University, and prior to that he also taught fifth and sixth grade in Salt Lake City, Utah, for seven years. Through international teaching experiences in Mozambique and Brazil, Ricks developed interests in cross-cultural studies and translations of Spanish and Portuguese texts. His articles have appeared in *The Dragon Lode*, *Literacy Research and Instruction*, *The Reading Teacher*, and *Literacy Today*.

Terri Robertson is a third-grade teacher at Citrus Grove Elementary School in DeLand, Florida, and a recent recipient of an MEd in educating for social justice at Stetson University.

Junko Sakoi, PhD, is the multicultural integration coordinator and teacher educator in the Department of Multicultural Curriculum and Instruction at Tucson Unified School District, Arizona. She has developed multicultural school curriculum and instruction with students, teachers, administrators, and communities. Her publications focus on Japanese pictorial texts and in- and out-of-school literacy, in addition to Kamishibai Japanese visual storytelling. She currently serves on the manuscript review board for *Bookbird: A Journal of International Children's Literature* and the Notable Books for a Global Society Award selection committee.

Kelly C. Scott is a visiting instructor at the University of North Florida, where she has taught literacy courses as well as methods for teaching social studies. Scott has served in multiple research analyst positions and in various teaching capacities in local public schools. Her research focus continues to be on students' motivation to read, with a specific attention on students' interest in reading nonfiction and informational texts.

Yoo Kyung Sung, PhD, is an associate professor in the Department of Language Literacy and Sociocultural Studies of University of New Mexico. She teaches a range of children's literature and literacy courses. Her most recent coauthored article with Junko Sakoi is entitled "Stories of the Ainu: The Oldest Indigenous People in Japanese Children's Literature" (2017) in the *Bookbird: A Journal of International Children's Literature*.

An avid reader, **Barbara A. Ward** is an associate clinical professor of literacy and children's literature at Washington State University in Pullman where she coordinates the elementary education program. She spent twenty-five years teaching in the public schools of New Orleans, Louisiana.

Lunetta M. Williams has taught first and third grades in public schools and continues to work with struggling readers at local elementary schools. Currently, she is professor and literacy program area leader at the University of North Florida. Williams teaches various undergraduate and graduate classes that focus on the importance of embedding diverse children's literature into the curriculum. Her research broadly focuses on mitigating the achievement gap among students from economically disadvantaged and economically advantaged backgrounds. More specific research interests include increasing students' reading achievement and motivation to want to read, independent reading time, and children's book selections.

Mario Worlds is a doctoral candidate at the University of Florida, studying literacy and literacy education. His research interests include education experiences of African American males. Additionally, he studies multicultural children's literature, exploring the cultural and social influences that shape learning and instruction of literature and literacy practices of underrepresented student populations. Worlds can be contacted at mareaszy@ufl.edu.

Vivian Yenika-Agbaw is professor of children's literature in the Department of Curriculum and Instruction at The Pennsylvania State University, University Park, where she teaches undergraduate and graduate courses in children's/adolescent literature. She has published numerous articles and authored/coedited several books including *Adolescents Rewrite their Worlds: Using Literature to Illustrate Writing Forms* (Rowman & Littlefield, 2015); *African Youth in Contemporary Literature and Popular Culture: Identity Quest* (Routledge, 2014); and *Fairy Tales with a Black Consciousness: Essays on Adaptations of Familiar Stories* (McFarland, 2013). She has taught children's literature in the Departments of Curriculum and Instruction and

English at state universities in Pennsylvania (Clarion and Bloomsburg), and has taught high school English abroad and in the United States. Yenika-Agbaw has served on several editorial boards and reviewed manuscripts for *Children's Literature in Education*, *Children's Literature*, and the *Journal of Children's Literature*. She is currently serving on the International Research Society for Children's Literature Board (2017–2019).

Terrell A. Young is professor of children's literature at the David O. McKay School of Education at Brigham Young University in Provo, Utah. Young is a coauthor or coeditor of numerous books on children's literature, including *Deepening Students' Mathematical Understanding with Children's Literature* (in press), *Children's Literature, Briefly* (2016), *Integrating Children's Literature Through the Common Core State Standards* (2015), and *Independent Reading: Creating Lifelong Readers* (2015). He previously taught in public elementary schools in Utah and Wyoming and private elementary schools in Venezuela. Young has served as president of the International Literacy Association Children's Literature and Reading Special Interest Group and the National Council of Teachers of English Children's Literature Assembly. He is currently the president elect of the US Board on Books for Young People. Young has enjoyed serving on numerous award committees, and was recently elected to serve on the 2019 Newbery Award selection committee.

www.ingramcontent.com/pod-product-compliance
Lightning Source LLC
Chambersburg PA
CBHW030142240426
43672CB00005B/232